"*Mapping Out Marketing* proves something that I would never have believed: academic writing can be interesting! The unique format forces the very best minds in marketing to ruthlessly cut to the chase and share their most novel and impactful ideas."
Michael Norton, Harvard Business School

"A very innovative and refreshing way to distill a wide range of topics in marketing!"
Jagdish N. Sheth, Charles Kellstadt Professor of Marketing, Emory University

Mapping Out Marketing

Sea-changes in society, technology, consumer expectations and our understanding of behavioral economics have caused us to rethink our understanding of the scope of knowledge required to navigate, analyze and shape consumer behavior.

You hold in your hand a field guide for this adventure. Ronald Hill and Cait Lamberton have gathered together the very top professors from around the world and invited them to share the beliefs, practices and wisdom that they have developed and honed across years and contexts.

Each of these luminaries shares personal stories and deep insights about the way that not only business works, but the way we, ourselves, navigate the world. These short contributions are contained in eight "destinations" that showcase overlapping and essential topics, ranging from technology to subsistence marketplaces, followed by unique questions that are answered by the material provided. The research described has helped the field understand the central role of exchange in marketing relationships, and how product features, pricing strategies, delivery mechanism and various communication modalities create or fail to produce functioning marketplaces around the world. In addition, it reminds us all of the need to continue to learn, to grow, and to share our knowledge – in whatever corner of the marketing world we find ourselves.

Ronald Hill, Ph.D. in business administration from the University of Maryland, is a Visiting Professor of Marketing and holds a Dean's Excellence Faculty Fellowship at the American University, Kogod School of Business. He has authored over 200 journal articles, books, chapters, and conference papers on topics that include impoverished consumer behavior, marketing ethics, corporate social responsibility, human development, and public policy.

Cait Lamberton is Associate Professor and Ben L. Fryrear Chair in Marketing at the University of Pittsburgh's Katz Graduate School of Business, where she researches and teaches consumer behavior and applied behavioral economics at the MBA and Ph.D. levels, in addition to providing consulting services in both government and the private sector.

Jennifer Swartz is a full-time MBA student at George Washington University with a focus on operations, strategy, and brand management. Prior to George Washington, she worked in Corporate Communications at Marsh & McLennan Agency in San Diego, overseeing various aspects of digital media strategy, branding, public relations, and non-profit fundraising efforts.

Mapping Out Marketing

Navigation Lessons from the Ivory Trenches

Edited by
*Ronald Hill, Cait Lamberton
and Jennifer Swartz*

LONDON AND NEW YORK

First published 2018
by Routledge
2 Park Square, Milton Park, Abingdon, Oxon OX14 4RN

and by Routledge
711 Third Avenue, New York, NY 10017

Routledge is an imprint of the Taylor & Francis Group, an informa business

© 2018 selection and editorial matter, Ronald Hill, Cait Lamberton and Jennifer Swartz; individual chapters, the contributors

The right of Ronald Hill, Cait Lamberton and Jennifer Swartz to be identified as the authors of the editorial material, and of the authors for their individual chapters, has been asserted in accordance with sections 77 and 78 of the Copyright, Designs and Patents Act 1988.

All rights reserved. No part of this book may be reprinted or reproduced or utilised in any form or by any electronic, mechanical, or other means, now known or hereafter invented, including photocopying and recording, or in any information storage or retrieval system, without permission in writing from the publishers.

Trademark notice: Product or corporate names may be trademarks or registered trademarks, and are used only for identification and explanation without intent to infringe.

British Library Cataloguing-in-Publication Data
A catalog record for this book is available from the British Library

Library of Congress Cataloging-in-Publication Data
Names: Hill, Ronald Paul, editor. | Lamberton, Cait, 1975– editor. |
Swartz, Jennifer, 1988– editor.
Title: Mapping out marketing : navigation lessons from the ivory trenches / edited by Ronald Hill, Cait Lamberton and Jennifer Swartz.
Description: Abingdon, Oxon ; New York, NY : Routledge, 2018. |
Includes bibliographical references and index.
Identifiers: LCCN 2018014783 (print) | LCCN 2018016000 (ebook) |
ISBN 9781315112602 (eBook) | ISBN 9781138082229 (hardback :
alk. paper) | ISBN 9781138082236 (pbk. : alk. paper)
Subjects: LCSH: Marketing. | Marketing—Management.
Classification: LCC HF5415 (ebook) | LCC HF5415 .M278 2018
(print) | DDC 658.8—dc23LC record available at
https://lccn.loc.gov/2018014783

ISBN: 978-1-138-08222-9 (hbk)
ISBN: 978-1-138-08223-6 (pbk)
ISBN: 978-1-315-11260-2 (ebk)

Typeset in Giovanni and Futura
by Florence Production Ltd, Stoodleigh, Devon, UK

Contents

Contributors	xii
Introduction	xvii

DESTINATION #1
Research and technology · 1

ENTRY #1	How do you stay on trend amidst the always-evolving world of digital marketing? *Andrew T. Stephen*	3
ENTRY #2	What role might bioscience play in helping us deepen our understanding of—and intervention in—human behavior? *Joseph W. Alba*	6
ENTRY #3	How can we conduct research that truly furthers our understanding of diversity, rather than reinforcing old models? *Jerome D. Williams*	9
ENTRY #4	How can you use models in a meaningful way for your market? *Greg Allenby*	12
ENTRY #5	Does "big data" have the right customer satisfaction answers? *Ronald Hill*	15
ENTRY #6	How can you capture data that reflects complex life decisions? *Fred M. Feinberg*	18
ENTRY #7	What are consumers' interactions with the Internet of Things and how does it affect marketing? *Donna L. Hoffman*	21

DESTINATION #2
Target markets and consumer behavior · 25

ENTRY #8 · Who are your consumers (really)? · 27
Americus Reed II

ENTRY #9 · How can you get to know the true identity of your target market? · 31
Craig J. Thompson

ENTRY #10 · What role does intuition play in consumers' decisions? · 34
Rebecca Walker Reczek

ENTRY #11 · Why does obligation play into consumers' behaviors and how can you prepare accordingly? · 37
Raj Raghunathan

ENTRY #12 · How can the sense of touch change consumer experience and response? · 40
Joann Peck

ENTRY #13 · Did you smell that? How scent affects the consumer experience · 43
Maureen Morrin

ENTRY #14 · How do you engage low-literate, low-income consumers and entrepreneurs in the marketplace? · 46
Madhu Viswanathan

DESTINATION #3
Branding · 49

ENTRY #15 · How do attitudes affect brands? · 51
Richard J. Lutz

ENTRY #16 · How can you strengthen communication effects to better your brand? · 54
Kevin Lane Keller

ENTRY #17 · How can marketers foster brand attachment? · 57
Andreas Eisingerich, Deborah J. MacInnis, and C. Whan Park

ENTRY #18 · When does your positional advantage pose challenges to success? · 60
Rebecca J. Slotegraaf

ENTRY #19 · How does your advertising affect consumers? · 63
Charles R. Taylor

ENTRY #20	How can you use your brand to help your consumers live better lives? *Deborah Roedder John*	66
ENTRY #21	Why hire someone who does not fit consumers' stereotypes? *Valerie S. Folkes*	68

DESTINATION #4
Enhancing the marketplace 71

ENTRY #22	Price competition, attraction effects, and line-extension effects: What are their hidden returns? *Timothy B. Heath*	73
ENTRY #23	What makes a new product successful? *Donald R. Lehmann*	76
ENTRY #24	What are the consequences for remedying risk? *Lisa E. Bolton*	79
ENTRY #25	Why do business relationships often fail and how can you turn that trend around? *Sandy D. Jap*	82
ENTRY #26	Is it better for us (and our consumers) to make decisions together or alone? *Cait Lamberton*	85
ENTRY #27	What steps can you take to create an inclusive marketplace? *Sonya A. Grier*	88
ENTRY #28	How can looking at the whole picture help you serve customers? *Michael K. Brady*	91

DESTINATION #5
Customer satisfaction 95

ENTRY #29	What do customers really want? *Michael Norton*	97
ENTRY #30	How do marketers bring back the voice of the customer? *Kelly D. Martin*	100
ENTRY #31	How does satisficing and justifying among consumers affect marketing? *James W. Gentry*	103

ENTRY #32 How can you better predict future consumer preferences
when consumers often have trouble doing so?   106
Rebecca Hamilton

ENTRY #33 How do your prices actually affect consumers?   109
Ryan Hamilton

ENTRY #34 How do you create the ultimate customer experience?   112
Kay Lemon

ENTRY #35 How do you measure service quality?   115
Valarie A. Zeithaml

DESTINATION #6
Consumer wellbeing   119

ENTRY #36 How can marketing spark change in consumer health?   121
Cornelia (Connie) Pechmann

ENTRY #37 What is the best strategy to employ when conducting
healthy food marketing?   124
Pierre Chandon

ENTRY #38 How does price influence food decision making?   127
Kelly L. Haws

ENTRY #39 What factors influence over-consumption and how
can marketers use this information to improve
customers' wellbeing?   130
Maura L. Scott

ENTRY #40 How do female mannequins impact consumers?   133
Jennifer J. Argo

ENTRY #41 How can marketing make prevention education
effective?   135
J. Craig Andrews

DESTINATION #7
Motivating change   139

ENTRY #42 How can you influence change and innovation?   141
Stacy Wood

ENTRY #43 What role do consequences play in motivating consumers?   144
George Loewenstein

ENTRY #44 How can you enhance consumer persuasion?   147
Punam A. Keller

ENTRY #45 How can you use negative associations to motivate
consumers? 150
Katherine White

ENTRY #46 How can you tap into consumers' surroundings to
influence their actions? 153
Juliano Laran

ENTRY #47 Does consumers' photo-taking enrich or impoverish
experience? 156
Gal Zauberman, Kristin Diehl, and Alix Barasch

ENTRY #48 What can you do to stay motivated throughout your
career? 159
Brian Wansink

DESTINATION #8
Marketing and the world at large 163

ENTRY #49 What does wisdom entail and how can it make you
a better marketer? 165
David Glen Mick

ENTRY #50 How is collaboration beneficial to you and your
business? 168
Julie L. Ozanne and Lucie K. Ozanne

ENTRY #51 How can you employ macromarketing to better
your business? 171
Clifford J. Shultz, II

ENTRY #52 How is sustainability changing the marketing world? 174
C. B. Bhattacharya

ENTRY #53 How does climate determine consumption and
culture? 177
Jagdish Sheth

ENTRY #54 How can you help children navigate market messages
as technology progresses? 180
Lan Nguyen Chaplin

ENTRY #55 What should students learn about marketing? 183
Leigh McAlister

Closing remarks 185
Index 189

Contributors

DESTINATION #1

Andrew T. Stephen—L'Oréal Professor of Marketing, Saïd Business School, University of Oxford

Joseph W. Alba—Distinguished Professor of Marketing, Warrington College of Business, University of Florida

Jerome D. Williams—Executive Vice Chancellor and Provost, Rutgers University-Newark

Greg Allenby—Helen C. Kurtz Chair in Marketing, Professor of Marketing, Professor of Statistics, Fisher College of Business, Ohio State University

Ronald Hill—Visiting Professor of Marketing and Dean's Excellence Faculty Fellow, American University, Kogod School of Business

Fred M. Feinberg—Handleman Professor of Marketing and Professor of Statistics, Ross School of Business and Department of Statistics, University of Michigan

Donna L. Hoffman—Louis Rosenfeld Distinguished Professor of Marketing, The George Washington University School of Business and the GW Center for the Connected Consumer

DESTINATION #2

Americus Reed II—The Whitney M. Young Jr. Professor, Professor of Marketing, The Wharton School, University of Pennsylvania

Craig J. Thompson—Churchill Professor of Marketing, Wisconsin School of Business, School of Journalism & Mass Communication, University of Wisconsin-Madison

Rebecca Walker Reczek—Associate Professor of Marketing, Fisher College of Business, Ohio State University

Raj Raghunathan—Professor of Marketing, University of Texas at Austin

Joann Peck—Associate Professor of Marketing, Wisconsin School of Business, University of WisconsinMadison

Mauren Morrin—Professor, Consumer Sensory Innovation Lab (CSIL), Temple University

Madhu Viswanathan—Diane and Steven N. Miller Professor, Subsistence Marketplaces Initiative, Marketplace Literacy Project, University of Illinois, Urbana-Champaign

DESTINATION #3

Richard J. Lutz—JCPenney Professor of Marketing, Warrington College of Business, University of Florida

Kevin Lane Keller—E.B. Osborn Professor of Marketing, Tuck School of Business, Dartmouth College

Deborah J. MacInnis—Professor of Marketing, Marshall School of Business, University of Southern California

C. Whan Park—Professor of Marketing, Marshall School of Business, University of Southern California

Andreas Eisingerich—Professor of Marketing, Imperial College, UK

Rebecca J. Slotegraaf—Professor of Marketing and Whirlpool Faculty Fellow, Kelley School of Business, Indiana University

Charles R. Taylor—John A. Murphy Professor of Marketing, Villanova School of Business

Deborah Roedder John—Curtis L. Carlson Chair in Marketing, Carlson School of Management, University of Minnesota

Valerie S. Folkes—Robert E. Brooker Chair and Professor of Marketing, Marshall School of Business, University of Southern California

DESTINATION #4

Timothy B. Heath—Professor Muma College of Business, University of South Florida

Donald R. Lehmann—George E. Warren Professor of Business, Columbia Business School

Lisa Bolton—Professor of Marketing, Smeal College of Business, The Pennsylvania State University

Sandy D. Jap—Sarah Beth Brown Endowed Professor of Marketing, Goizueta Business School, Emory University

Cait Lamberton—Ben L. Fryrear Chair and Associate Professor in Marketing, Katz Graduate School of Business, University of Pittsburgh

Sonya A. Grier—Professor of Marketing, American University

Michael K. Brady—The Carl DeSantis Professor, Florida State University

DESTINATION #5

Michael Norton—Harold M. Brierley Professor of Business Administration, Harvard Business School

Kelly D. Martin—Dean's Distinguished Research Fellow and Associate Professor of Marketing, College of Business, Colorado State University

James W. Gentry—Maurice J. and Alice Hollman College Professor, University of Nebraska-Lincoln

Rebecca Hamilton—Michael G. and Robin Psaros Chair in Business Administration and Professor of Marketing, McDonough School of Business, Georgetown University

Ryan Hamilton—Associate Professor of Marketing, Goizueta Business School, Emory University

Kay Lemon—Accenture Professor, Boston College

Valarie A. Zeithaml—The David S. Van Pelt Family Distinguished Professor, University of North Carolina at Chapel Hill

DESTINATION #6

Cornelia (Connie) Pechmann—Professor of Marketing, The Paul Merage School of Business, University of California Irvine

Pierre Chandon—L'Oréal Chaired Professor of Marketing, Innovation and Creativity, INSEAD

Kelly L. Haws—Associate Professor of Marketing and Chancellor's Faculty Fellow, Owen Graduate School of Management, Vanderbilt University

Maura L. Scott—Madeline Duncan Rolland Associate Professor of Business Administration, Florida State University

Jennifer J. Argo—Carthy Professor of Marketing, University of Alberta

J. Craig Andrews—Professor and Kellstadt Chair in Marketing, Marquette University

DESTINATION #7

Stacy Wood—Executive Director, Consumer Innovation Consortium, Poole College of Management, North Carolina State University

George Loewenstein—Herbert A. Simon Professor of Economics and Psychology, Carnegie Mellon University

Punam A. Keller—Charles Henry Jones Professor of Management, Tuck School of Business, Dartmouth College

Katherine White—Professor, Marketing and Behavioral Science, Sauder School of Business, University of British Columbia

Juliano Laran—Professor of Marketing, University of Miami School of Business Administration

Kristin Diehl—Associate Professor of Marketing, Marshall School of Business, University of Southern California

Gal Zauberman—Professor of Marketing, Yale School of Management

Alix Barasch—Assistant Professor of Marketing, Stern School of Business, New York University

Brian Wansink—John S. Dyson Professor of Marketing, Cornell University

DESTINATION #8

David Glen Mick—Robert Hill Carter Professor of Commerce, McIntire School of Commerce, University of Virginia

Lucie K. Ozanne—Associate Professor of Marketing, University of Canterbury

Julie L. Ozanne—Professor of Marketing, University of Melbourne

Clifford J. Shultz, II—Charles H. Kellstadt Professor of Marketing, International Fellow, Harvard-Fulbright Economics Teaching Program

CB Bhattacharya— Zoffer Chair of Sustainability and Ethics, Katz Graduate School of Business, University of Pittsburgh

Jagdish Sheth—Charles H. Kellstadt Professor of Marketing, Goizueta Business School, Emory University

Lan Nguyen Chaplin—Associate Professor of Marketing, University of Illinois at Chicago

Leigh McAlister—Professor, Ed and Molly Smith Chair in Business Administration, McCombs School of Business, University of Texas at Austin

Introduction

Most readers of this book are well-acquainted with both self-help and business practice books—two genres that increasingly blur together. A quick perusal of self-help books presents us with a consistent formula: state the problem, give the solution, and tell numerous stories about its origin and/or application.

These works are clearly well-meaning, with most having at least some value to readers who face similar situations in their professional lives. Some of these volumes become "bibles" for managers, who seek to use their lessons on a regular basis. Others tell their stories, leaving the messages to be forgotten.

Regardless, the "telling" is often long and anecdotal. There are times when reading the front and back covers reveal the principal takeaways, making further reading uneventful. Could the entire lesson(s) be contained in a well-written paragraph or two? If so, is the rest of the book primarily justification for the higher sticker price?

On the other hand, academics devote entire careers to developing scholarly pieces that could, if widely read, profoundly change lives and marketing practices. Unfortunately, writing for peer-reviewed journals does not lend itself to easy reading, and perhaps for good reason: scientific journals prioritize rigor, and with that necessarily comes a certain level of abstraction and nuance. But how do we get these pearls of wisdom out of the ivory trenches and into your hands?

It is with these insights that we edited this book. Jokingly, we considered the title, *"The one-minute manager who moved my cheese to the tipping point."* Clearly tongue-in-cheek, but you get the picture: our goal is to give you accumulated wisdom across a wide-swath of topics and experts rather than one idea recycled over-and-over, again-and-again. And our goal is to do it in a way that is practical, readable and—we hope—enjoyable.

To this end, we asked fifty-five top marketing academics who teach undergraduate, MBA, and Ph.D. students at the finest colleges and universities around the world to contribute to this volume. We are fortunate to know them personally, and their work has set the stage for research on the most complex and critical topics of our age.

We asked an essential question of these great minds: what would you like the world to know about your research that they may not understand by reading one of your academic articles or its translation in a self-help book? Not just a singular point, but a reader-friendly gestalt of a lifetime of work that every business student or executive should know to be more successful. They responded eagerly to this call, especially knowing that we only wanted 500 words.

The research they describe has helped the field understand the role of technology, analysis, product features, pricing strategies, delivery mechanisms, consumer experience and identity and various communication modalities create or fail to create functioning marketplaces around the world. Breathtaking in its scope, they are the thinkers who drive the field.

The result is the book you now hold.

And that was our introductory 500 words. (We held ourselves to the same limit.)

To get you started, here is a brief outline of what comes next, emphasizing what you will gain from your investment:

- Each offering is contained in one of eight "destinations" that showcase overlapping and essential topics, followed by a unique question that is answered by the material provided.
- The professor whose work is showcased gives her or his 500-word articulation on this matter, also providing some research references and web-based materials if you desire more depth.
- We close with a brief "gestalt of these gestalts," in which we attempt to crystallize these vistas.

The time and money you have invested here is not just an investment in yourself: all author proceeds will support scholarships for doctoral level educations of underrepresented persons through the American Marketing Association's Foundation at a diverse set of universities and colleges. We are thankful for the way that they have enriched our field, and delighted to pay forward that contribution in this small way.

So, welcome to the book; you might think of it as a cocktail party with about fifty brilliant people—swapping stories, telling you about the ideas that have ignited their imaginations and their work, and sharing challenges they see on the horizon. Grab a snack, make a drink, and stay awhile; we are glad you are here, and we cannot wait to share the experience with you.

Sincerely, Ron & Cait

DESTINATION #1

Research and technology

ENTRY #1

How do you stay on trend amidst the always-evolving world of digital marketing?

Andrew T. Stephen

L'Oréal Professor of Marketing, Saïd Business School, University of Oxford

Over the last 15–20 years, the marketing landscape has undoubtedly changed. These changes began, of course, with the introduction of the internet, and then continued as the internet matured and evolved. The rise of connected mobile devices and social media, more recently, have rapidly advanced the field of marketing, particularly on the practice side. And it keeps changing, so much so that the past often is not worth following when new and interesting things are always coming out. How do marketing academics and practitioners grapple with this? How do we, as a critical business discipline, attempt to make sense of the always-new marketing landscape (and consumers' behaviors within new, technology-enabled marketing channels)? Is it feasible to follow the past, at least somewhat, to help us understand the future?

These and related issues are considered by Lamberton and Stephen (2016) and Stephen (2016). Put simply, these review articles conclude that there is much left to understand about the digital marketing world and where it is heading. Additionally, they call for all types of marketers to embrace the uncertainty of the digital future by adopting a broader scope when it comes to research on digital behaviors, platforms, and channels.

Notwithstanding the always-changing nature of the digital landscape, we can use what we know from the past to help us understand the future because of consumer psychology. For example, Bart, Stephen, and Sarvary (2014) study mobile advertising field experiment data to work out which types of mobile ads work and why. They use theory from psychology on persuasion and information processing to make sense of their empirical findings that, perhaps surprisingly, the highest-performing mobile ads (based on increasing brand favourability and purchase intent) are those for utilitarian products that require higher-involvement in the purchase decision process. Even though mobile ads change, these findings are rooted in human psychology and shed light on how people process tiny bits of marketing information displayed on their relatively small smartphone screens.

Another example of this approach is Chae, Stephen, Bart, and Yao (2017). This article reports a study of hundreds of seeded word-of-mouth (WOM) marketing campaigns for specific products and looks at the WOM-generating consequences of these seeding efforts. Interestingly, however, we considered both the intended consequences of generating more WOM about a campaign's focal product among non-seed consumers, and the unintended consequences of generating more—or potentially less—WOM about (i) other products from the same brand as the focal product and (ii) other products in the same category as the focal product but from competitors. These unintended consequences are referred to as brand and category WOM spillover effects, respectively. It is important to consider unintended consequences, particularly in the relatively new and increasingly "hot" space of seeded marketing campaigns, which is otherwise known as influencer marketing. We find that seeding increases WOM about the seeded focal product (as would be expected), but decreases WOM about other products from the same brand and other products in the same category but from other brands. That is, we find negative brand and category WOM spillover effects. We explain these using psychological theories related to how people construe stimuli (in this case, products and brands) and argue that a marketer's act of seeding a specific product with consumers can lead to lower-level construals and focused thinking, which suppresses brand- and category-related thoughts cued by the initial stimulus (the focal product). Despite the ongoing evolution of influencer marketing, these findings help marketers know what to expect based on an understanding of the underlying consumer psychology.

In summary, it is true that if one is to study the newest, cutting-edge digital marketing phenomena then they cannot realistically expect to always be following the past. However, sometimes we can rely on the fact that human psychology is changing at a much slower pace, such that we find ourselves in a situation where the more things change, the more they stay the same.

TAKEAWAYS

- Digital marketing is constantly evolving but that does not mean that everything is always new.

- We can turn to fundamentals, such as consumer psychology, to help us understand the new while building on the old.

- To advance marketing theory and practice in the context of digital channels/platforms, we should take more of a psychology-based perspective.

REFERENCES

Bart, Yakov, Andrew T. Stephen, and Miklos Sarvary (2014), "Which Products Are Best Suited to Mobile Advertising? A Field Study of Mobile Display Advertising Effects on Consumer Attitudes And Intentions," *Journal of Marketing Research*, 51 (3), 270–285.

Chae, Inyoung, Andrew T. Stephen, Yakov Bart, and Dai Yao (2017), "Spillover Effects in Seeded Word-of-Mouth Marketing Campaigns," *Marketing Science*, 36 (1), 89–104.

Lamberton, Cait and Andrew T. Stephen (2016), "A Thematic Exploration of Digital, Social Media, and Mobile Marketing Research's Evolution from 2000 to 2015 and an Agenda for Future Research," *Journal of Marketing*, 80 (6), 146–172.

Stephen, Andrew T. (2016), "The Role of Digital and Social Media Marketing in Consumer Behavior," *Current Opinion in Psychology*, (August), 1017–1021.

ENTRY #2

What role might bioscience play in helping us deepen our understanding of—and intervention in—human behavior?

Joseph W. Alba

Distinguished Professor of Marketing, Warrington College of Business, University of Florida

Free will is the defining issue of humanity. For millennia, it has been the province of philosophy, but lay beliefs about human agency broadly penetrate social policy. The present is a rousing time to examine the intersection of agency and policy due to developments in neuroscience and genetics that offer causal models of human traits and behavior. These causal models naturally adhere to the scientific view that all causality is fundamentally physical. However, they clash with the public's view of agency, which skews toward the non-corporeal. The research question for marketing concerns whether the popularization of bioscience will bridge the chasm between science and lay belief. The implications are profound, not just for consumer theory and our view of human nature but also for pragmatic questions surrounding personal welfare, social equality, and the macro-economy.

Consider the extensively examined consumer trait of self-control. A strong and non-corporeal view of human agency might explain the inclination to engage in self-defeating consumption as under the individual's control and attributable to an absence of will or character. However, research shows that:

1. Self-control during childhood is a powerful predictor of adult health, wealth, and criminality.
2. Children's self-control is influenced by the level of adversity in their environment.
3. An adverse childhood environment has neurological effects that govern adult self-control.

This research suggests a very different model of self-defeating consumption—a model that views transgressors as suffering from a debilitating physiological condition stemming from exogenous factors beyond their control.

From a consumer-policy perspective, pervasive beliefs about human agency place constraints on the ability of policy makers to enact autonomy-threatening rules. These constraints render libertarian paternalism as the least objectionable but not the most effective route to enhanced public welfare. From a social-policy perspective, research shows that childhood interventions that prevent neurological damage or ameliorate its effects provide a sizeable social return on investment. However, government intervention requires investment, investment requires public consent, and public consent is dependent on the perceived necessity of intervention versus the sufficiency of self-control, determination, and other traits that are inherent in the autonomous-person view of humanity. From the perspective of practice, acceptance of physical causation will favour interventions that alter the body rather than the spirit.

TAKEAWAYS

- Consumer research takes place almost entirely within the framework of social science. Our theories will be better informed by inclusion of a physiological perspective.

- Despite their good intentions, marketing researchers do not exert a large influence on public policy and exert almost no influence on the dissemination of findings from the natural sciences. Rigorous examination of how consumers react to scientific developments can address both failings.

- Consumers' preferences for competing paths to self-improvement are guided by their beliefs about the causes

Bioscience and understanding human behavior **7**

of their deficiencies—as are competing remedies. Improved choices and market offerings depend on better understanding of those causes.

REFERENCES

Williams, L. E. and T. Andrew Poehlman (2017), "Conceptualizing Consciousness in Consumer Research," *Journal of Consumer Research*, 44 (2), 276–282.

Zheng, Yanmei, Stijn M. J. Van Osselaer, and Joseph W. Alba (2016), "Belief in Free Will: Implications for Public Policy," *Journal of Marketing Research*, 53 (December), 1050–1064.

ENTRY #3

How can we conduct research that truly furthers our understanding of diversity, rather than reinforcing old models?

Jerome D. Williams

Executive Vice Chancellor and Provost, Rutgers University-Newark

For decades, consumer research on racial and ethnic minority groups had assumed homogeneity, i.e., each group represented a monolithic group. For example, the few studies on African Americans focused on samples of lower income, usually urban consumers, and then generalized those results to all African Americans. When comparisons were made with the "general" population, those samples typically were taken from white middle-class neighborhoods. It was argued that the ghetto community was the most typical setting for the black community.

Fortunately, research on multicultural consumers has advanced significantly beyond those early efforts to understand these segments, but in my opinion, not far enough. First, the number of studies is still relatively negligible. For example, several content analyses of studies in our primary marketing journals reveal that research on racial/ethnic minority segments and issues received virtually no attention, e.g., only 2.5 percent of the total number of articles had a racial or ethnic minority focus and only 2.0 percent of the total number of subjects were identified as racial or ethnic minorities.

As the population of the United States grows ever more diverse, it becomes questionable whether concepts and theories developed and tested on the majority consumer group (i.e., White, Euro-Americans) can be appropriately applied to ethnic minority consumer groups (e.g., African-Americans, Hispanics, Asian-Americans, etc.). These multicultural groups not only demonstrate significant differences in terms of household compositions, values, lifestyles, self-perceptions, aspirations, etc., from the majority group, but also great diversity within each group.

One way to enrich our understanding of multicultural consumers is to move away from the traditional thinking of viewing these groups as monolithic segments to be compared to the general population of White consumers. Essentially, we need to adapt the methods and approaches that have been used by race and ethic scholars in other fields, such as psychology, sociology, public health etc., and accept diversity within as a legitimate approach. This contrasts with the approach often advocated by editors and reviewers to use Caucasians as the comparison or control group necessary to understand the findings from research on an ethnic minority group. This approach reflects the Cultural Deviant Model, which characterizes differences between groups as deviant and inferior.

I would argue that researchers studying racial and ethnic consumer groups should not feel compelled to accept the traditional logic that Caucasians are the most logical or necessary contrast against which racial and ethnic groups should be compared. In certain cases, this might be appropriate, depending on what concepts and behaviors are being examined. However, I would challenge researchers to ask different questions beyond "what are the differences between Whites and specific racial and ethnic groups?" Investigating within-group differences offers researchers an opportunity to identify the magnitude of heterogeneity within each group. Furthermore, within-group investigations can significantly advance our understanding of multicultural marketing by providing information that is lost in the traditional between-group comparisons.

TAKEAWAYS

- Do not assume that finding differences between the White majority group and multicultural segments are the most interesting.

- In pursuing "diversity-within" research, be prepared to push back with editors and reviewers who suggest that you need a "control" group to legitimize your findings.

- Recognize some sub-segments within a racial group may exhibit behavior closer to the White-majority population than other sub-segments within that same racial group.

REFERENCES

Bone, Sterling A., Glenn L. Christensen, and Jerome D. Williams (2014), "Rejected, Shackled, and Alone: The Experience of Systemic Restricted Consumer Choice among Minority Entrepreneur Consumers," *Journal of Consumer Research*, August, 41 (2), 451–474.

Whitfield, Keith E., Jason C. Allaire, Rhonda Belue, and Christopher L. Edwards (2008), "Are Comparisons the Answer to Understanding Behavioral Aspects of Aging in Racial and Ethnic Groups?" *Journal of Gerontology*, 63B (5), 301–308.

Williams, Jerome D., Wei-Na Lee, and Geraldine R. Henderson (2008), "Diversity Issues in Consumer Psychology Research," in Curtis P. Haugtvedt, Paul Herr, and Frank Kardes (eds.), *Handbook of Consumer Psychology*, Hillsdale, NJ: Lawrence Erlbaum, 877–912.

ENTRY #4

How can you use models in a meaningful way for your market?

Greg Allenby

Helen C. Kurtz Chair in Marketing, Professor of Marketing, Professor of Statistics, Fisher College of Business, Ohio State University

The error term of a model is the catch all for things not modelled correctly, including model misspecification, omitted variables, and errors encountered in recording the data. Regression models include an additive error component that allows the regression model to reconcile any observation, however deviant, to the assumed model structure. The advantage of this is that it is difficult to "break" the regression model. The disadvantage is that its ability to accommodate any observation makes it difficult to claim that certain observations are unreasonable or that certain values of the model coefficients are inadmissible.

Consider the additive error assumption in a choice model. If the error is assumed to be normally distributed, with support on the real number line, then the resulting model of choice cannot have alternatives that can dominate other alternatives. While this might not seem like a big deal, it is when the model of choice is applied to many choice alternatives on the scale found in any retail establishment. A choice model with additive errors involving, say, 50 choice alternatives and 50 error terms leaves a lot of wiggle room for explaining choices—i.e., confidence intervals on model parameters are not very narrow and the model does not have much "bite."

Now consider the effect of the additive error assumption in models of consideration and choice. One way of approaching this two-stage model is to first think about the probability of consideration for an alternative and then the probability of choice, with each specified with its own additive error term. Having additive errors in the consideration model means that there is some positive probability that any of the choice alternatives would be considered— i.e., that all alternatives would be considered to some degree. But models of consideration mean that some alternatives should be screened out of evaluation and not evaluated for choice. The assumption of an additive error implies that all brands are considered to some extent, and as a result the model doesn't matter as much as it should.

When investigating the demand and price of goods in a competitive market, the presence of market prices that are not too extreme implies that the price elasticity is likely in the elastic range. Similarly, when investigating expenditure allocation decisions on the part of the manager, the presence of positive allocations to multiple options implies the presence of diminishing marginal returns to expenditures. Assuming that consumers are rational in that they prefer lower prices to higher prices, given all else is equal, this means that pricing effects go in one direction only. For none of these examples is an additive error structure in the model appropriate as some parameter values are not permissible, and some behaviors should have zero likelihood of occurring.

The solution to the additive error assumption is to consider employing structural and non-compensatory models of behavior, where hard constraints are present and some behavior is not explainable. These models require thought as to how errors enter into the model specification, providing sharper predictions about what matters to consumers. The error term specification matters if you want your model to matter.

TAKEAWAYS

- Employ a structural and non-compensatory behavior model to address the additive error assumption.

REFERENCES

Aribarg, Anocha, Thomas Otter, Daniel Zantedeschi, Greg M. Allenby, Taylor Bentley, David J. Curry, Marc Dotson, Ty Henderson, Elisabeth Honka, Rajeev Kohli, Kamel Jedidi, Stephas Seiler, and Wxin Wang (2018), "Advancing Non-Compensatory Choice Models in Marketing," *Customer Needs and Solutions*, 5 (1), 82–92.

Gilbride, Timothy J. and Greg M. Allenby (2004), "A Choice Model with Conjunctive, Disjunctive, and Compensatory Screening Rules," *Marketing Science*, 23 (3), 391–406.

ENTRY #5

Does "big data" have the right customer satisfaction answers?

Ronald Hill

Visiting Professor of Marketing and and Dean's Excellence Faculty Fellow, Department of Marketing, American University, Kogod School of Business

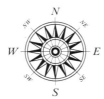

Many marketing professionals believe that, when consumers buy their products, they are satisfied, especially if they continue to purchase the same goods or services over time. Even most theoretical conceptions of customer satisfaction suggest that people are contented if they buy repeatedly. The underlying idea is simple economic logic: consumers only exchange money for products if the products are worth more than the money.

However, is it possible that these persons believe that your offering is the least objectionable alternative (if there are any others)? Consider the time I was stuck in traffic for several hours because of an accident on a then-closed highway. Someone with cold water (it was summer) walked by and offered bottles that sold in bulk for 25 cents for an asking price of $10. When queried by me how he arrived at that price, he simply stated: "I have got it and you do not."

You may think this is a one-time, unique set of circumstances, but consider people without transportation in impoverished communities; are they happy buying produce at twice the price for half the quality of their more affluent counterparts just because they lack adequate transportation to discount retailers? How does awareness of these options impact their feelings of satisfaction?

Maybe it is time to rethink what we mean by customer satisfaction. With "big data" the playing field has shifted in profound ways. Marketers have more information about their customers on a timely basis, allowing firms to make real-time adjustments to their product offerings. Yet while we know more, these data reflect who buys what rather than the totality of benefits to purchasers in both the short and long-term. Consider information that tells us women between 25 and 45 who are of African American descent, and single mothers of two or more children living in urban areas are highly likely to purchase our goods and services. Are their underlying rationales for why clear? We can intuit their reasons and even ask for clarification, but marketers may still miss the mark.

Our goals for comprehending how our products serve customers should shift from who buys what to how products fit into the constellation of items purchased that impact the quality of consumers' lives. For example, if these women tend to buy more fast food than other cohorts, can we assume that they do so out of choice rather than necessity? Might these mothers use calorie-dense, cheaper foods to ensure their children eat regularly but still realize that long-term consumption has a negative impact on diet choices and health? Such an understanding can help marketers make more informed decisions that serve them and their customers in positive ways.

This perspective of our customers and organizations will make us more responsive as well as more responsible. Marketers can be more responsive since they now look at the impacts of products more systemically, capturing the fuller picture of the role of goods and services in the lives of the people they serve. They are also more responsible because they recognize the positive and negative consequences of using their products that supersede simple decisions to buy or not buy.

TAKEAWAYS

- Simple purchase behavior may not necessarily signal customer satisfaction. Marketers need to consider customer needs relative to alternatives available in the market.

- "Big data" have considerable value, but resulting information may not fully capture the range of customer reactions to your products.

- Knowing your customers may require a systemic understanding of their constellation of goods and service and how your products support need satisfaction in the longer term.

REFERENCES

Hill, Ronald Paul, Justine Rapp, and Michael Capella (2016), "Antiservice as a Guiding Maxim: Tough Lessons from a Maximum Security Prison," *Journal of Service Research*, 19 (1), 57–71.

Hill, Ronald Paul and Kelly D. Martin (2014), "Broadening the Paradigm of Marketing as Exchange: A Public Policy and Marketing Perspective," *Journal of Public Policy & Marketing*, 33 (Spring), 17–33.

Bennett, Aronte and Ronald Paul Hill (2013), "The Impact of Disparate Levels of Marketplace Inclusion on Consumer-Brand Relationships," *Journal of Public Policy & Marketing*, 32 (Spring), 16–31.

ENTRY #6

How can you capture data that reflects complex life decisions?

Fred M. Feinberg

Handleman Professor of Marketing and Professor of Statistics, Ross School of Business and Department of Statistics, University of Michigan

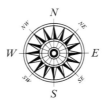

Over the past few decades, decision researchers—psychologists, statisticians, economists, sociologists—have fashioned a comprehensive, if patchwork, theory of *how people make choices*. It goes roughly like so: faced with an impending decision, we cobble together an index of each option's attractiveness, then select the seemingly best among them. We do this with lots of missing or inaccurate information, under time, financial, and cognitive constraints, and without knowing much for sure about the future. Worse, we seldom get feedback about "what might have been:" passed-up menu entrées, books we never got to, colleges courses we missed out on, etc. It is a wonder we get anything right, or believe we do.

This framework performs well, statistically, when a lot of information can be placed into a model meant to replicate how people "weight" it all. Indeed, Google, Amazon, and other web Oracles depend on it: "If you are buying this mystery novel, you will just love that immersion blender." Throw in some sophisticated machine learning, and one can even transcribe speech, search the web, and return answers in natural language. Modelling magic!

All this works far less well when we are simply navigating our way, vague goal in hand, through a novel landscape. When considering a new profession, looking for love, or hoping to create a nest egg, things get trickier: we start in a state of near-ignorance, engage in jumpy exploratory behavior, and refine our own preferences, learning lessons along the way. Decisions about spouses, jobs, education, and large-scale purchases are among the most critical in life: how can researchers begin to unravel how they are made?

One answer is through Activity Data: digital bread crumbs we leave behind when we google, click, roam, and interact with others in ways that leave a trail. Consider what is arguably one's most important choice: a long-term relationship partner (or deciding not to seek one). In years past, sociologists and marketers could ask people what was critical for them, or study successful vs. unsuccessful couplings. The advent of online dating has gifted researchers with arrestingly granular data regarding what we believe we want: qualities we search for, whom we "click" or swipe, those we write to (or ignore), even what we confide. In other words, a cornucopia of highly varied information on every stage of relationship formation. Such digital trails now exist for every major (and most minor) choices we make, allowing for the first time a fine-grained account of how people navigate their professional, business, personal, and emotional lives.

There is an old saying that *not everything that counts can be counted*. While this is still true—can we ever hope to measure the effects of a kind word or wry smile?—we have for the first time a literal trove of information unveiling the process of people trying to achieve their goals and dreams. All we, as researchers, need do is find a way to drink it all in, synthesize it, and divine what it is trying to tell us.

TAKEAWAYS

- The really important Big Data for Marketing and Social Science is Activity Data.

- Complex Life Decisions require more than putting all available information into a model.

- We can for the first time hope to unravel the process of people hoping to achieve their goals and dreams.

REFERENCES

Bruch, Elizabeth, Fred Feinberg, and Kee Yeun Lee (2016), "Extracting Multistage Screening Rules from Online Dating Activity Data," *Proceedings of the National Academy of Sciences*, 113 (38), 10530–10535.

Bruch, Elizabeth and Fred Feinberg (2017), "Decision Making Processes in Social Contexts," *Annual Review of Sociology*, 43, 207–227.

Dellaert, Benedict G. C., Joffre Swait, Wiktor L. Vic Adamowicz, Theo A. Arentze, Elizabeth E. Bruch, Elisabetta Cherchi, Caspar Chorus, Bas Donkers, Fred M. Feinberg, and Anthony A. J. Marley (2017), "Individuals' Decisions in the Presence of Multiple Goals," *Customer Needs and Solutions*, 1–14.

Marley, Anthony A. J. and Joffre Swait (2017), "Goal-based Models for Discrete Choice Analysis," *Transportation Research Part B: Methodological*, 101, 72–88.

Swait, Joffre, and Anthony A. J. Marley (2013), "Probabilistic Choice (Models) as a Result of Balancing Multiple Goals," *Journal of Mathematical Psychology*, 57 (1–2), 1–14.

ENTRY #7

What are consumers' interactions with the Internet of Things and how does it affect marketing?

Donna L. Hoffman

Louis Rosenfeld Distinguished Professor of Marketing, The George Washington University School of Business and the GW Center for the Connected Consumer

The consumer Internet of Things (IoT) has the potential to revolutionize consumer experience. Recent research has developed a framework for evaluating how consumers are likely to experience their interactions with smart devices. One finding from this research is that four specific types of consumer experience are likely to emerge during consumers' interactions with smart devices. These include enabling experiences of agentic self-extension and communal self-expansion, and constraining experiences comprised of agentic self-restriction and communal self-reduction. One unique aspect of this emerging research is the idea that in order to fully understand the kinds of experiences that are likely to emerge for consumers in the IoT, we should recognize that smart devices are also likely to have their own emergent enabling and constraining experiences.

While the idea that smart devices can have experiences might at first seem a bit odd, it starts to make sense when you consider that smart devices are different from traditional products because they possess the ability to act (agency), the ability to function independently without consumer intervention (autonomy), and are able to implement communication and decision making with other smart devices and with consumers (authority). Because smart devices have the capacity to interact with other entities, they can enable other devices or consumers or constrain other devices or consumers. However, even though smart devices engage in interactions on their own and from these interactions their experiences emerge, these experiences are very different from consumer experiences.

A particularly interesting aspect of this perspective is how smart device experience might be perceived by consumers. Because consumers can never have direct access to the exact properties of a smart device, they can only interact with it in the context of the consumer-device assemblage of which both the consumer and the smart device are a part. So, experience is constructed from that interaction. It has been proposed that consumers can speculate about object experience using a trio of tools including ontography, object-oriented anthropomorphism, and carpentry. In this approach, smart device experience is evaluated not from our own human-centric perspective, but by speculating how the smart device might perceive things from its own, (non-human) perspective.

There are a number of implications of these concepts for consumer research. We can view a smart device as an "intelligent agent" which itself is a consumer that can be understood and marketed to directly. For example, object consumers can have the equivalent of affective responses, such as when smart devices are satisfied only when they are achieving their goals. Object consumers can also participate in consumption such as when Amazon's Dash Replenishment service allows washing machines to re-order laundry detergent on their own when they are running low. Object consumers can also make decisions such as when, through a smartphone app, smart refrigerators can display the inside of the refrigerator to a consumer at the grocery store and suggest products and recipes contingent on what she already has at home.

The consumer IoT is beginning to revolutionize consumption and consumer experience in a broad and growing range of consumer-facing categories. Object experience and how consumers can access it can contribute to a fuller understanding of the nature of consumer behavior, and its expanding domain, in complex, interactive environments like the IoT.

TAKEAWAYS

- Consumer-smart device assemblages will emerge from all the bottom-up interactions that are developed by individual consumers for their unique situations, not from a small set of five or six top down use cases (e.g. "safety" or "security"). Marketers should employ a bottom-up approach when marketing smart devices that encourages consumers to figure out for themselves through their own interactions how best to use different devices.

- Habitual repetition involves performing routine behaviors over and over again until they become habits. When different smart devices—lights, thermostats, apps, appliances—and consumers interact over time in a predictable way, emerging research predicts that the behavior resulting from habitual repetition will stabilize usage patterns, encouraging greater use and discouraging churn.

- As consumers continue to interact with their smart devices and new experiences emerge, these experiences have the potential to outweigh privacy concerns. Understanding these experiences will give marketers insight into what features consumers value enough to trade off some aspects of their privacy. These experiences are likely to involve personalization. For example, marketers like Amazon and Wal-Mart are currently testing IoT systems involving smart locks and cameras that will allow a delivery person to enter one's home and put away groceries or leave packages inside the home when the consumer is not at home.

REFERENCES

Hoffman, Donna L. and Thomas P. Novak (2018), "Consumer and Object Experience in the Internet of Things: An Assemblage Theory Approach," *Journal of Consumer Research*, forthcoming.

Hoffman, Donna L. and Thomas P. Novak (2017), "Send 'Her' My Love: A Circumplex Model for Understanding Relationship Journeys in Consumer-Smart Object Assemblages," *Center for the Connected Consumer Working Paper*, August 8. Available at SSRN: https://ssrn.com/abstract=3059093

Hoffman, Donna L. and Thomas P. Novak (2016), "How to Market the Smart Home: Focus on Emergent Experience, Not Use Cases," *Center for the Connected Consumer Working Paper*, January 15. Available at SSRN: https://ssrn.com/abstract=2840976

DESTINATION #2

Target markets and consumer behavior

ENTRY #8

Who are your consumers (really)?

Americus Reed II

The Whitney M. Young Jr. Professor, Professor of Marketing, The Wharton School, University of Pennsylvania

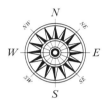

A consumer's sense of who they are is complex. It is not one static thing as some early research assumed. Instead, a single person's identity is dynamic. It can consist of many elements. We are endowed with some. We willingly adopt others. For example, you could see yourself as an American, a father, an athlete, a professor, a Republican, a musician, etc.

How do we juggle these different parts of who we are? A modern multi-dimensional perspective has profound implications for how consumers navigate their world, what they choose to do (and not do). In fact, identity is often at the core of how consumers can generate their sense of happiness, meaningfulness and life satisfaction. Marketing managers and public policy advocates should take heed.

Every consumer is a walking set of multiple target markets. What is interesting here is that the different identities a consumer may have can become strongly associated with specific attitudes, emotions and behaviors. Each one can be a source of tremendous fulfilment and meaningfulness. This is where the well-informed brand manager or public policy advocate can have an "ah-ha" moment. Understand that different identities may have different and even opposite implications as to how that consumer may behave while they are in that role. Think of it as complexity not inconsistency. Think of it as an opportunity to understand that the consumer may think, feel and do different things because that identity is a proscription to guide their judgment and decision making.

This is more nuanced than just "personality" or even "psychographics." This is a call to understand the complex identities of a specific group of consumers for whom you want to connect.

A consumer's identity can strengthen or weaken over time. Any individual identity can be reinforced or diluted by feedback from the environment. This is an opportunity for brand marketers and public policy advocates. In the age of social media, consumers now have direct ways to be reinforced in the identities they value (e.g., giving and receiving direct feedback on their social media platforms). Our research shows that brands need to be very careful. Brands need to be partners who are a part of the consumers' conversations and not companies trying to sell products. The key construct is "authenticity" whereby brand managers need to have a credible record of accomplishment in supporting that key identity. Public policy advocates need to understand that behaviors are key inputs to identity. Do you want consumers to exercise more, smoke less? Make that identity a strong (I am an athlete) or weak (I am a smoker) component of that consumer's sense of whom they are.

A consumer's multiple identities may be in conflict from time to time. Consumers often have conflict amongst the different identities that they want to hold. This is a consequence of having complexity. On the one hand, research shows that the more identities a person has, the more they are better able to maintain self-esteem in the face of failure(s) associated with any particular identity. On the other hand, the more identities a person has the more chances that intra-identity conflict may arise. For example, imagine a man who suddenly takes on the identity of "father." He may find this new identity in conflict with a previous sense of who he was. Therein lies an opportunity for brands and public policy advocates to help that consumer "reduce" the conflict. This may have been the reason why a category of automobiles called "SUVs" was created. A sports utility vehicle is essentially a mini-van for men who wish to see themselves as accommodating the new requirements of being a "dad" with the importance of maintaining a masculine aspect of who they are.

Identity loyalty is the key concept for creating affiliation and powerful behavioral change. Perhaps the most important insight regarding identity is the idea that if a product, brand, service, or behavior becomes internalized as part of a consumer's sense of identity, then identity loyalty is the result. Our research finds that identity loyalty is a powerful motivator. Consumers who align their identities with the identities associated with brands, products, services, and behaviors become one-man, one-woman marketing departments (free of charge!). They will defend those brands because an attack on the brand is an attack on themselves. Identity loyalty is an intense internal switching cost because it is more than just "liking" something. Instead, it is "attachment to" something. It makes consumers willing to pay more, wait longer and sacrifice more to maintain those brands, products, services and behaviors that are linked to their identity. Identity loyalty then, is a brand's buffer. It makes perfect sense. Getting a consumer to switch from a brand, product, or service to another, is asking them to change who they are. That is a tall order. That is also an opportunity to create and change behavior.

Very few choices in life do not have an implication for how you see yourself and how the outside world sees you. Therefore, if we accept the premise that a consumer's identity is multi-faceted, then we must understand what is in it and how and why it changes (or does not) over time. A deep understanding of these issues allows for extremely powerful behavioral change and deep insights into what drives happiness and life satisfaction.

TAKEAWAYS

- Every consumer has several identities that are a part of who they are. Each one is a unique target market that can connect with a product, brand, service, organization or behavior.

- People may behave very differently when they are enacting different identities. Do not misidentify this as "inconsistency"— instead understand this complexity and understand what identities a particular group of consumers have adopted, and help them reduce any conflict between identities.

- There are very concrete things you can do to reinforce behaviors associated with a good identity (e.g., being a healthy person with a healthy lifestyle) and dilute behaviors associated with a bad identity (e.g., being a smoker). You have to connect the dots through consistent reinforcement and messaging.

- There is an opportunity to connect brands and behaviors to a person's identity in such a way that the consumer becomes 'identity loyal' to the product or the action. This means that they become a one-man, one-woman free marketing department. An evangelist of that brand, product, service or behavior.

Who are your consumers (really)? **29**

REFERENCES

Reed II, Americus and Mark R. Forehand (2016), "The Ebb and Flow of Consumer Identities: The Role of Memory, Emotions and Threats," *Current Opinion in Psychology*, 10 (August), 94–100.

Reed II, Americus, Mark R. Forehand, Stefano Puntoni, and Luke Warlop (2012), "Identity-based consumer behavior," *International Journal of Research in Marketing*, 29 (4), 310–321.

Reed, II Americus, Joel B. Cohen, and Amit Bhattacharjee (2009), "When Brands Are Built from Within: A Social Identity Pathway to Liking and Evaluation," in D. MacInnis, C. W. Park, and J. Priester (eds.), *Handbook of Brand Relationships*, M. E. Sharpe, 124–150.

ENTRY #9

How can you get to know the true identity of your target market?

Craig J. Thompson

Churchill Professor of Marketing, Wisconsin School of Business, School of Journalism & Mass Communication, University of Wisconsin-Madison

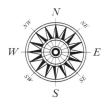

Know thy consumer! It would be hard to find a more accepted truism in marketing. A seemingly infinite, decades-spanning array of books, articles, news reports, class room lectures, and business strategy meetings have focused on the task of understanding "consumers," and satisfying their fickle wants and needs. But, what if this marketing pursuit of the elusive "consumer" manifests a fundamental misconception? Consider, if you will, this question: on your tombstone, would you want your epitaph to proclaim that you "were a truly informed consumer?" When we reflect upon the events and activities that make our lives meaningful, our role of being "consumers"—that is, economic agents who enter into exchange relationships to acquire goods and services—is an incidental contributor but never an end to itself. Rather, people buy goods and services in order to accomplish particular identity goals, whether it be enhancing the happiness and well-being of their children (thereby enacting an ideal of being a good parent), forming social bonds with others—what Cova (2007) refers to as the linking value of products and services—or transforming their identity in desired ways.

As an example of this latter case, Thompson and Üstüner (2015) studied women who invested their identities in becoming derby grrrls.

For these women, the sport of roller derby instilled a sense of performative confidence in their bodies (regardless of size or shape) and to adopt a more assertive orientation in their relationships to others. Whereas they had (socialized) tendencies to be self-sacrificing and deferential to their domestic partners and male co-workers, their experiences as derby grrrls helped them to attain a better balance between their own interests and those of others and to be more proactive in ensuring that their voices were heard and respected. These identity transformations took time—and lots of arduous training—as the skills and habits they formed through practicing the sport slowly became incorporated into their every demeanour. This transformative process also required significant commitments of time and money that many of our participants, several of whom were struggling to make ends meet, had in very short supply. However, their choices were not driven by economic calculations. Rather, their actions were motivated by the identity value offered by this network of experiences, social connections, and acquired skills. In the process of becoming derby grrrls, these women did also periodically act as consumers—for example, buying roller skates, protective gear, costume apparel, insurance and so forth. However, reducing their identity goals and corresponding activities to these particular economic exchanges would be akin to explaining the enduring aesthetic and cultural value of the *Mona Lisa* by reference to the price that da Vinci paid for his oil paints and canvas.

Researchers who study in a subfield of consumer behavior known as Consumer Culture Theory (CCT) (see Arnould and Thompson 2005) argue that "consumers" are better conceived as social actors who pursue their identity goals through consumption practices. From this perspective, consumption practices are always embedded in a shifting web of social relations, cultural meanings, and material conditions that organize a person's life and the broad range of social roles he/she enacts across various life settings (i.e., the workplace, the home and domestic life, leisure spaces, and yes, retail settings). This network of relations, rather than a specific good or service, is the key to understanding a person's purchase preferences, brand loyalties, and "needs" broadly defined as the resources that enable them to enact their identity goals. To generate enduring loyalty and commitment, marketers need to understand how their offerings can facilitate the identity goals and enrich the social connections among the people who choose to co-creatively integrate a brand into their lives (also see Coskuner-Balli and Thompson 2013; Cova and Cova 2002; Fournier 1998; Holt and Cameron 2010).

TAKEAWAYS

- Do not assume that social actors are interested in your brand. Rather, they are interested in their life goals and seeking out resources that would allow them to realize those ends. Your brand has to demonstrate that it can be a positive contributor to their identity projects.

- You cannot understand why a person buys one brand than another without placing those decisions and preferences in the context of his/her identity goals and social networks.

- Social actors are above all else social. People use products and services as way to build connections with others. And people most value connections that allow them to realize their identity goals. One essential task of marketing is finding ways to make a brand an integral resource to these identity-constituting relational networks and activities.

REFERENCES

Arnould, Eric and Craig J. Thompson (2005), "Consumer Culture Theory (CCT): Twenty Years of Research," *Journal of Consumer Research*, 31 (4), 868–882.

Coskuner-Balli, Gokcen and Craig J. Thompson (2013), "The Status Costs of Subordinate Cultural Capital: At-Home Fathers' Collective Pursuit of Cultural Legitimacy Through Capitalizing Consumption Practices," *Journal of Consumer Research*, 40 (1), 19–41.

Cova, Bernard and Veronique Cova (2002), "Tribal Marketing: The Tribalisation of Society and Its Impact on the Conduct of Marketing," *European Journal of Marketing*, 36 (5/6), 595–620.

Cova, Bernard, Robert Kozinets, and Avi Shankar (2007), *Consumer Tribes*, Oxford: Butterworth-Heinemann.

Fournier, Susan (1998), "Consumers and Their Brands: Developing Research Theory in Consumer Research," *Journal of Consumer Research*, 24 (4), 343–353.

Holt, Douglas and Douglas Cameron (2010), *Cultural Strategy: Using Innovative Ideologies to Build Breakthrough Brands*, Oxford: Oxford University Press.

Thompson, Craig J. and Tuba Üstüner (2015), "Women Skating on the Edge: Marketplace Performances as Ideological Edgework," *Journal of Consumer Research*, 42 (2), 235–265.

ENTRY #10

What role does intuition play in consumers' decisions?

Rebecca Walker Reczek

Associate Professor of Marketing, Fisher College of Business, Ohio State University

As consumers, we have to make a lot of decisions, often when we do not have complete information. Research in consumer behavior shows that consumers often rely on their intuitions to infer or "guess" what the missing information might be. This can often be very functional, as it allows consumers to make quick, easy decisions. For example, consumers tend to assume that unhealthy foods are not tasty or that expensive foods are healthier, simply because they have come over time to believe that health and taste are negatively correlated and that health and price are positively correlated. Intuitions like these about the relationships between product attributes are often called lay theories. People's lay theories are their common sense explanations of how the world works, and people have lay theories about everything from how the natural world works to these types of product-specific lay theories.

When we are making decisions about products, we often do not think about the fact that these broad intuitions do not apply universally and simply make inferences of missing attributes using the intuitions that, in turn, affect our judgements and choices. The influence of our intuitions can be so strong that participants in one study who were told that a mango lassi (a milkshake-like drink from India) was a healthy snack thought it tasted worse than participants who consumed the exact same food but were told that it was an unhealthy snack.

While product-specific lay theories may be true in some cases (which is likely how consumers have come to believe in them over time), they are not necessarily true in all cases, which is when consumers are led astray. Just because the newest fad ingredient for a "healthy" diet is being sold at a higher price point does not mean it actually is an important part of a healthy diet for the average consumer. Similarly, there are many examples of foods that are both healthy and tasty. Problems arise when consumers over apply lay theories that may be true in some situations to making judgments and decisions in all situations.

So what does this mean for consumers? We are most likely to rely on our intuitions rather than seeking out more objective facts when we are in a hurry or when we are just not motivated to think very carefully about the information we are encountering. We also tend to rely on intuitions more when we lack expertise in a given area. If you want to avoid applying these lay theories in situations when you should not, then that means taking the time to think through decisions carefully and educating yourself on areas that are particularly important to you (e.g., by going to third party sources to learn about products like Consumer Reports).

For managers, this means that you have a battle on your hands if your product violates a strongly held consumer lay theory. Consider the commonly held belief that sustainable products are not strong and effective. Many consumers will assume that a green cleaning product is not as good as a non-green product. The onus is on the manufacturer to provide the consumer with information ensuring that it is. In other words, do not leave information about the product's strength as "missing" information that consumers have to infer based on their intuition. Instead, offer a "strength guarantee" so that consumers do not fall prey to their intuition and avoid your product all together.

TAKEAWAYS

- Consumers have lay theories about the relationships between certain product attributes (e.g., unhealthy = tasty, healthy = expensive, sustainable = less effective) that are often over-applied to situations where they are not true.

- Consumers are more likely to rely on these lay theories when making decisions under time pressure or when their general knowledge in the product category is low.

Intuition and consumers' decisions   **35**

- Managers with products that violate these intuitions should not leave attribute information as "missing," instead providing information that stops consumers from relying on their lay theories.

REFERENCES

Deval, Hélène, Susan P. Mantel, Frank R. Kardes, and Steven S. Posavac (2013), "How Naive Theories Drive Opposing Inferences from the Same Information," *Journal of Consumer Research*, 39 (April), 1185–1201.

Haws, Kelly, L., Rebecca Walker Reczek, and Kevin Sample (2017), "Healthy Diets Make Empty Wallets: The Healthy = Expensive Intuition," *Journal of Consumer Research*, 43 (April), 992–1007.

Luchs, Michael, Rebecca Walker Naylor, Julie R. Irwin, and Rajagopal Raghunathan (2010), "The Sustainability Liability: Potential Negative Effects of Ethicality on Product Preference," *Journal of Marketing*, 74 (September), 18–31.

Raghunathan, Rajagopal, Rebecca Walker Naylor, and Wayne D. Hoyer (2006), "The 'Unhealthy = Tasty' Intuition and Its Effects on Taste Inferences, Enjoyment, and Choice of Food Products," *Journal of Marketing*, 70(4), 170–184.

ENTRY #11

Why does obligation play into consumers' behaviors and how can you prepare accordingly?

Raj Raghunathan

Professor of Marketing, McCombs School of Business, University of Texas at Austin

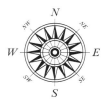

In the story of Tom Sawyer, the protagonist famously tricks his friends into painting his fence for him. How? By denying them the opportunity to paint the fence until they beg and bribe him. Tom capitalized on an important insight: being denied the opportunity to do something makes us all the more eager to do it. Or, conversely, when something feels like an obligation, it becomes less enjoyable. This may be why we find work —which feels like an obligation—to be unenjoyable!

Does this insight translate to consumption contexts? For example, do consumers find "work-related"—or "functional"—products to be less enjoyable (or "hedonic"), and vice versa?

Findings from several studies appear to suggest so. Take one study by Raghunathan et al. (2006) which looked at the perceived correlation (in consumers' minds) between the healthiness and tastiness of food. Participants in the study, who had been invited to a house warming party, were asked to sample, among other things, some Mango lassi. Under the pretext that the caterers of the food items were interested in participants' opinions about their fare. The lassi was portrayed as either healthy (to about half the participants) or unhealthy (to the rest). After consuming the lassi, participants were then asked to rate its tastiness.

As predicted, those led to believe that it was healthy found it to be less tasty and vice versa. Other studies have confirmed that products with superior functional features are automatically assumed to be less hedonic.

The fact that consumers appear to subscribe to, what may be called, a "more fun = less functional" intuition, is a problem for marketers. By making a product more emotionally appealing, marketers may inadvertently signal that it does not perform as well. For example, by making their earphones more colorful and attractive, Sony may be turning away consumers interested in sound quality. And since functional features may, overall, be considered more important than hedonic features (e.g., Chitturi et al. 2007, 2008), enhancing a product's hedonic appeal may have an unintended detrimental effect on its success.

One way out of this quandary is to deliberately degrade a product's hedonic features. Some firms appear to be doing exactly this. Listerine—the mouthwash—stings even though it does not need to. Why? Because consumers believe that it is more effective in killing germs when it stings than when it does not.

There is, however, a problem with this strategy: degrading a product's hedonic quality may make it seem functionally superior, but it makes the product instinctively less appealing. This leads to an important question: is there a way of enhancing a product's hedonic features while simultaneously signaling superior—or at least acceptable levels of—functionality?

There is. This way is to explicitly extoll these products' superior functionality even while conveying, perhaps only implicitly, its hedonic quality. Several firms follow this strategy, with Apple being perhaps the most obvious example. Apple's products are famously hedonically pleasing. But notice how their advertisements, while subtly highlighting their products' hedonic features, also explicitly convey their functional features—such as the lightness of their laptops, or the memory capacity of their iPods. By doing so, Apple effectively negates the negative inferences about functionality that consumers could be drawing. This may be an important reason for the company's fantastic success.

TAKEAWAYS

- Consumers subscribe to the lay-belief that a hedonically superior (that is "good looking") product is likely to be functionally inferior (that is, not as effective).

- One way to negate this lay-belief is to deliberately degrade the product's hedonic features. This is a good strategy in product categories (e.g., fertilizers, medicine) where functional benefits are far more important than hedonic ones.

- An alternative strategy is to explicitly extoll the (hedonically superior) product's functional quality so as to negate the influence of the "more fun = less functional" lay-belief.

REFERENCES

Raghunathan, Rajagopal, Rebecca W. Naylor, and Wayne Hoyer (2006), "The 'Unhealthy = Tasty' Intuition and its Effects on Taste-Inferences, Enjoyment and Choice of Food Products," *Journal of Marketing*, 70 (4), 170–184.

Chitturi, Ravi, Rajagopal Raghunathan, and Vijay Mahajan (2007), "Form Vs. Function: How the Intensities of Specific Emotions Evoked in Functional versus Hedonic Tradeoffs Mediate Product Preferences," *Journal of Marketing Research*, 44 (4), 702–714.

Chitturi, Ravi, Rajagopal Raghunathan, and Vijay Mahajan (2008), "Delight by Design: The Role of Hedonic Vs. Utilitarian Benefits," *Journal of Marketing*, 72 (3), 48–63.

ENTRY #12

How can the sense of touch change consumer experience and response?

Joann Peck

Associate Professor of Marketing, Wisconsin School of Business, University of Wisconsin-Madison

When browsing through a store, you reach out to feel the soft texture of a sweater as you pass by a display. Will this action make you more likely to impulsively purchase the sweater? And, would this touch also increase the amount you would pay for the sweater? Research with my colleagues tell us that the answer is yes to both of these questions!

As you shop, you may touch various products to obtain product information, such as the texture or the weight of a sweater. In fact, the sense of touch, or haptics, is better than any other sense at obtaining certain types of information. These include weight, texture, and temperature. A product category that varies in a meaningful way on one of these attributes will generally encourage touch. For example, consumers are motivated to touch a sweater as compared to a book, as a book does not vary in a meaningful way in any of the attributes at which touch excels.

In addition to product differences that may motivate touch, our research shows that some individuals are more motivated to touch compared to others, an individual difference termed need-for-touch (NFT). Higher NFT individuals are those people ripping open packaging in stores in order to feel the products. This group is also less likely to shop online or through a catalog, where touch is unavailable. They are also more confident in their decisions and less frustrated when they can touch a product prior to purchase.

But touch is not just limited to trying to evaluate a product. Besides using touch to obtain product information, in some cases, you may simply enjoy the touch, even if you have no purchase goal. Maybe a soft or silky texture encouraged you to reach out and touch. Or you pick up a book in order to read more about the plot or the author. What was surprising to us is that even touch that does not result in additional information can still effect you.

In our research, we discover that any type of touch, for any type of individual can lead to an increase in unplanned or impulse purchase. Why is this? We find that merely touching an object leads to a greater sense of psychological ownership. Psychological ownership is distinct from legal ownership and is the feeling that something is "mine." For example, if you frequent a coffee shop, you may have a seat that you feel is yours, even if you do not actually own the seat. And, we value more objects that we own, even psychologically own. So, touching a product makes you feel more psychological ownership of that product, which increases your willingness to pay for that product as well as the likelihood you may impulsively purchase it.

Also, be cautious of trial periods. The longer you interact with a product, the more psychological ownership you will feel and the more you will pay for that product. What about shopping online? We find that imagining touching a product and imagining owning a product can also increase a feeling of ownership and your willingness to pay. There is a positive side. If we feel psychological ownership over an object, we are likely to take better care of it. So, be careful what you touch!

TAKEAWAYS

- Be careful what you touch! Mere touch can lead to a feeling of ownership, impulse purchases and an increase in willingness to pay.

- When shopping online, simply imagining touch or imagining ownership can also increase both your feelings of ownership and your willingness to pay.

REFERENCES

Peck, Joann, Victor Barger, and Andrea Webb (2013), "In Search of a Surrogate for Touch: The Effect of Haptic Imagery on Psychological Ownership and Object Valuation," *Journal of Consumer Psychology*, 23 (2), 189–196.

Peck, Joann and Terry L. Childers (2006), "If I Touch it I Have to Have it: Individual and Environmental Influences on Impulse Purchasing," *Journal of Business Research*, 59, 765–769.

Peck, Joann and Suzanne Shu (2009), "The Effect of Mere Touch on Perceived Ownership," *Journal of Consumer Research*, 36 (3), 434–447.

Peck, Joann and Jennifer Wiggins (2006), "It Just Feels Good: Consumers' Affective Response to Touch and Its Influence on Persuasion," *Journal of Marketing*, 70 (October), 56–69.

ENTRY #13

Did you smell that? How scent affects the consumer experience

Maureen Morrin

Professor, Consumer Sensory Innovation Lab (CSIL), Temple University

Have you ever wondered whether scent improves your memory? Researchers in marketing have wondered about this and tested the notion empirically. The majority of published research regarding this question suggests that, yes, smelling certain odors can indeed improve your ability to remember things such as brand names, product attributes, and packaging.

However, the effect of scent on improving your ability to remember aspects of the marketplace depends, in part, on how much time has evolved since you were exposed to information in a scented environment. For example, if you view various brands of product packaging while smelling a pleasant odor, and you then try to recall or recognize such stimuli shortly thereafter (e.g., five minutes later), the presence of an ambient scent at the time of exposure and retrieval helps but just a little bit in aiding your memory.

If you try to remember such information after a longer time delay, however, such as one day later or even two weeks later, then the effectiveness of the scent as a memory aid becomes much more evident. The importance of a time delay in demonstrating scent's effect on memory performance was directly tested in Krishna and Morin (2010). Here we found very little drop-off over time in consumers' ability to remember advertised product attribute information as much as two weeks after exposure to scented (versus unscented) products. In contrast, there was considerable drop-off in consumers' ability to remember information about unscented products after a two-week delay.

Collectively, this research stream suggests that scent can indeed improve your memory, but it may act more like a tortoise than a hare, with its strongest effects emerging over time.

Another interesting aspect of the scent research in marketing shows that scent present at the time of information exposure (i.e., time of encoding) is what most aids memory performance. Scent present at the time of retrieval appears to play a smaller role. In this way, scent can also be thought of as a "peg" for storing new information into our long-term memory banks. It is less effective as a retrieval cue—although it does help to a certain extent. The research also suggests that information learned in association with a scent is relatively immune to interference from information learned later.

TAKEAWAYS

- Scent's ability to improve your memory emerges most strongly after a time delay.

- Thus, if you wish to remember something for the long term, seeing it or thinking about it in the presence of a pleasant odor might indeed be helpful.

- The scent can be either present in the atmosphere (ambient) or emanating from a product, in order to have a positive effect on memory.

- The memory-aiding effects of scent are relatively impervious to interference from later-learned information.

REFERENCES

Krishna, Aradhna, May Lwin, and Maureen Morrin (2010), "Product Scent and Memory," *Journal of Consumer Research* 37 (June), 57–67.

Krishna, Aradhna, Maureen Morrin, and Eda Sayen (2014), "Smellizing Cookies and Salivating: A Focus on Olfactory Imagery," *Journal of Consumer Research*, 41 (June), 18–34.

Lwin, May O., Maureen Morrin, and Aradhna Krishna (2010), "Exploring the Superadditive Effects of Scent and Pictures on Verbal Recall: An Extension of Dual Coding Theory," *Journal of Consumer Psychology*, 20 (3), 317–326.

Madzharov, Adriana, Lauren Block, and Maureen Morrin (2015), "The Cool Scent of Power: Effects of Ambient Scent on Consumer Preferences and Choice Behavior," *Journal of Marketing*, 79 (1), 83–96.

Morrin, Maureen and Jean-Charles Chebat (2005), "Person-Place Congruency: The Interactive Effects of Shopper Style and Mall Atmospherics on Consumer Expenditures," *Journal of Service Research*, 8 (2), 181–191.

Morrin, Maureen, Aradhna Krishna, and May O. Lwin (2011), "Is Scent-Enhanced Memory Immune to Retroactive Interference?" *Journal of Consumer Psychology*, 21 (3), 354–361.

Morrin, Maureen and S. Ratneshwar (2000), "The Impact of Ambient Scent on Evaluation, Attention and Memory for Familiar and Unfamiliar Brands," *Journal of Business Research*, 49 (2), 157–165.

Morrin, Maureen and S. Ratneshwar (2003), "Does It Make Sense to Use Scents to Enhance Brand Memory?" *Journal of Marketing Research*, 40 (1), 10–25.

ENTRY #14

How do you engage low-literate, low-income consumers and entrepreneurs in the marketplace?

Madhu Viswanathan

Diane and Steven N. Miller Professor, Subsistence Marketplaces Initiative, Marketplace Literacy Project, University of Illinois, Urbana-Champaign

Two decades ago, I observed a group of low-income, low-literate consumers shopping. I was left with one feeling—the things I take for granted, as someone with education and financial resources. Tasks that I do not give any thought to can take so much effort for someone who is low-literate—like finding where a product is located or computing the final price after discounts or totaling a shopping basket. Having enough money at the counter can be cause for celebration, and falling short, cause for despair. How someone thinks, feels, and behaves can be fundamentally different as a result of low literacy and low income. Those of us with the most education or financial resources are, in a sense, the least qualified to understand low-literate, low-income consumers. Even basic concepts we take for granted like nutrition, health, what it means to be a customer, or how a business operates can be abstractions for those living in the immediate world and lacking resources and education. At the same time, people may be materially poor but socially or relationally rich.

Our journey had begun, as we developed an area called subsistence marketplaces. We aimed to understand consumers, entrepreneurs, and marketplaces across the world at the micro level of how people think, feel, and act in their life circumstances. In turn, we aimed to be bottom-up in using the insights for designing and implementing solutions. Subsistence means barely making ends meet at the bottom range of low income. And marketplaces (not markets) mean we need to understand these pre-existing environments in order to design solutions, rather than view them as new markets for existing products and policies.

Being bottom-up means allowing experiences on the ground to influence our thinking, involving people from the communities or employees at the boundaries of the organization and learning from them, and so on. Being bottom-up is as important as top-down, particularly in poverty contexts that managers are unfamiliar with, contexts that are filled with uncertainties, and myriad cultural and geographic differences. For instance, it is not sufficient to understand the consumer—the community and the larger context are just as important to understand. And managers have to design solutions for settings where usage situations and uses of products are very difficult if not impossible to anticipate.

We have detailed what bottom-up means for developing innovations and enterprise models. As an example, we talk of sustainable products, with a notion of sustainability in terms of people, planet, and profit. But this is top-down, and it is just as important to understand what people living in subsistence are trying to sustain—such as culture, livelihood, and so forth as they survive, relate, and try to grow. Understanding what is good for the community and the household is also important from the perspective of the organization. We have designed a range of learning experiences and educational material to understand the bottom-up approach and about subsistence marketplaces.

To engage in the marketplace as consumers and entrepreneurs, we believe there are three important elements—financial resources, access to markets, and what we call marketplace literacy—i.e., skills and knowledge, self-confidence, and awareness of rights as customers and as entrepreneurs. We have developed a unique marketplace literacy program now offered in four continents that addresses the difficulties low-literate, low-income individuals have. Our program focuses on deeper understanding of the marketplace or know-why, as a basis for know-how and know-what. We concretize, localize, and socialize the education.

Finally, understanding and designing solutions for subsistence marketplaces, can, in turn, provide the foundation for solutions for all contexts. Innovating in resource-constrained environments with many uncertainties can lead to solutions for higher income settings as well.

Low-literate and low-income consumers

TAKEAWAYS

- Suspend assumptions and learn about subsistence marketplaces bottom-up. Spend time in the field just for the purpose of learning. Have in-depth conversations without filters with those at the bottom of society. Observe life circumstances.

- Consider how you can be more bottom-up as an individual and as an organization, to complement being top-down. Think of exercises and processes that emphasize the bottom-up.

- Understand what is good for the household and the community. Incorporate this understanding into your organization.

REFERENCES

Homepage: www.business.illinois.edu/~madhuv/homepage.html

Non-profit website: www.marketplaceliteracy.org

Subsistence Marketplaces Initiative: https://business.illinois.edu/subsistence

Viswanathan, Madhubalan (2016), *Bottom-Up Enterprise: Insights from Subsistence Marketplaces*, eBookpartnership, eText, and Stipes.

Viswanathan, Madhubalan (2013), *Subsistence Marketplaces*, eBookpartnership, eText, and Stipes.

Viswanathan, Madhubalan, S. Gajendiran, and R. Venkatesan (2008), *Enabling Consumer and Entrepreneurial Literacy in Subsistence Marketplaces*, Dordrecht, Netherlands: Springer.

Viswanathan, Madhubalan, Jose Antonio Rosa, and James Harris (2005), "Decision Making and Coping by Functionally Illiterate Consumers and Some Implications for Marketing / Management," *Journal of Marketing*, 69 (1), 15–31.

Viswanathan, Madhubalan, Jose Antonio Rosa, and Julie Ruth (2010), "Exchanges in Marketing Systems: The Case of Subsistence Consumer Merchants in Chennai, India," *Journal of Marketing*, 74 (May), 1–18.

Viswanathan, Madhubalan and Srinivas Sridharan (2012), "Product Development for the BoP: Insights on Concept and Prototype Development from University-Based Student Projects in India," *Journal of Product Innovation Management*, 29 (1), 52–69.

Viswanathan, Madhubalan, Srinivas Sridharan, Robin Ritchie, Srinivas Venugopal, and Kiju Jung (2012), "Marketing Interactions in Subsistence Marketplaces: A Bottom-Up Approach to Designing Public Policy," *Journal of Public Policy and Marketing*, 31 (2), 159–177.

DESTINATION #3

Branding

ENTRY #15

How do attitudes affect brands?

Richard J. Lutz

JCPenney Professor of Marketing, Warrington College of Business, University of Florida

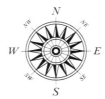

The attitude construct has enjoyed decades of research, initially in social psychology and subsequently in marketing and consumer research. An attitude is generally defined as a learned predisposition to respond in a consistently favourable or unfavourable manner to some object. The object can be a person, an idea, etc. In marketing research, much attention has focused on consumers' attitudes toward brands and advertising.

A particularly influential theory of attitude that originated in psychology (e.g., Fishbein and Ajzen 1975) is the multi-attribute model (MAM). Emanating from an expectancy x value tradition, the MAM asserts that brand attitudes can be predicted (and, importantly, diagnosed) by assessing the brand on a relatively small number of salient attributes, weighted by the evaluative properties (or, alternatively, importance) of each attribute. In addition to being intuitively appealing, the MAM has a track record of strong predictive power, proving useful in predicting consumer brand choice in a variety of contexts. Even more importantly, the MAM offers diagnostic insight into the underlying basis for brand attitudes (i.e., perceptions of a brand's want-satisfying properties), thereby yielding implications for attitude change strategies. The MAM thus informs both product design and promotional strategies.

A second influential stream of attitude research has examined consumer attitudes toward advertising (sometimes referred to as ad likeability). This research has demonstrated that consumer attitudes toward an advertisement "rub off" on the brand being promoted, especially under low involvement processing conditions. Ad attitudes, typically measured using Semantic Differential scales, are strong predictors of brand attitude and purchase intention. Under higher involvement conditions, ad attitude has a dual effect. Structural equation analysis has demonstrated that in addition to the direct relationship between ad attitude and brand attitude, ad attitude is positively related to brand perceptions that in turn predict brand attitude. This represents an indirect effect of ad attitude on brand attitude. Importantly, related applied research has found that standard copy-test measures of ad likability are strongly predictive of ad campaign sales performance.

The concept of advertising likability has become more important than ever over the past two decades as the media landscape and consumer markets have fragmented. The advent of digital video recorders and their ad skipping capabilities, as well as internet ad blocking software, have made it far more difficult to initiate and maintain consumer attention and engagement. The lessons learned through research on attitudes toward advertising suggest that advertising must be entertaining as well as informative in order to be successful. Of course, the entertainment aspect is no longer limited to traditional mass media advertising. It also encompasses product placement, guerrilla marketing, event marketing, etc. Ultimately, a brand's promotional activities must create favourable brand associations that increase brand attitudes, strengthen brand equity, and encourage greater customer loyalty.

TAKEAWAYS

- Investigating brand attitudes using a multi-attribute model approach is useful not only for predicting consumer brand choice but also for diagnosing the perceptions underlying those attitudes.

- The positive attitude generated by an advertisement "rubs off" on brand attitudes and purchase intentions both directly and indirectly by enhancing audience acceptance of ad claims.

- Brand managers and their promotional partners (e.g., ad agencies) should generally aim to construct advertisements that not only communicate relevant brand information but do so in an engaging fashion.

REFERENCES

Brown, Steven P. and Douglas M. Stayman (1992), "Antecedents and Consequences of Attitude toward the Ad: A Meta-analysis," *Journal of Consumer Research*, 19 (June), 34–51.

Fishbein, Martin and Icek Ajzen (1975), *Belief, Attitude, Intention and Behavior: An Introduction to Theory and Research*, Reading, MA: Addison-Wesley.

Haley, Russell I. and Allan L. Baldinger (2000), "The ARF Copy Research Validity Project," *Journal of Advertising Research*, 40 (November), 114–35.

Lutz, Richard J. (1975), "Changing Brand Attitudes Through Modification of Cognitive Structure," *Journal of Consumer Research*, 1, 49–59.

MacKenzie, Scott B., Richard J. Lutz, and George E. Belch (1986), "The Role of Attitude Toward the Ad as a Mediator of Advertising Effectiveness: A Test of Competing Explanations," *Journal of Marketing Research*, 23 (2), 130–43.

MacKenzie, Scott B. and Richard J. Lutz (1989), "An Empirical Examination of the Structural Antecedents of Attitude Toward the Ad in an Advertising Pretesting Context," *Journal of Marketing*, 53 (April), 48–65.

ENTRY #16

How can you strengthen communication effects to better your brand?

Kevin Lane Keller

E.B. Osborn Professor of Marketing, Tuck School of Business, Dartmouth College

For brand equity to be built, it is critical that communication effects created by advertising be linked to the advertised brand. Often, such links are difficult to create. TV ads in particular do not "brand" well. There are a number of reasons why:

- Competing ads in the product category can create interference and consumer confusion as to which ad goes with which brand.
- "Borrowed interest" creative strategies and techniques—humor, music, special effects, sex appeals, fear appeals, etc.—may grab consumers' attention, but result in the brand being overlooked in the process.
- Delaying brand identification or providing few brand mentions may raise processing intensity but direct attention away from the brand.
- Limited brand exposure time in the ad may allow little opportunity for elaboration of existing brand knowledge.
- Consumers may not have any inherent interest in the product or service category or may lack knowledge of the specific brand.
- A change in advertising strategy may make it difficult for consumers to easily relate new information to existing brand knowledge.

For all these reasons, advertising may "succeed" in the sense that communication effects are stored in memory, yet "fail" at the same time in that these communication effects are not accessible when critical brand-related decisions are being made. To address this problem, three potentially effective strategies, grounded in my past academic research, are brand signatures, advertising retrieval cues, and coordinated media.

- Brand Signatures. Perhaps the easiest way to increase the strength of brand links to communication effects is to create a more powerful and compelling brand signature. The brand signature is the manner by which the brand is identified in a TV or radio ad or displayed within a print ad. The brand signature must creatively engage the consumer and cause him or her to pay more attention to the brand itself and, as a consequence, increase the strength of brand associations created by the ad. An effective brand signature often dynamically and stylistically provides a seamless connection to the ad as a whole. For example, MasterCard's famous "Priceless" ads end with the two ovals making up their logo coming together in a way to reinforce the message or creative theme from that particular ad execution.
- Advertising Retrieval Cues. Another effective tactic is to use advertising retrieval cues—visual or verbal information uniquely identified with an ad that is evident when consumers are making any product or service decision. The purpose is to maximize the probability that consumers who have seen or heard the cued ad will retrieve the communication effects stored in long-term memory. Ad retrieval cues may consist of a key visual, a catchy slogan, or any unique advertising element that serves as an effective reminder to consumers. For example, Eveready has featured a picture of its pink bunny character on packages of Energizer batteries to reduce consumer confusion with Duracell.
- Coordinated Media. Print (or display) and radio ad reinforcement of TV ads (in which the video and audio components of a TV ad serve as the basis for the respective type of ads) can be an effective means to leverage existing communication effects from TV ad exposure and more strongly link them to the brand. Cueing a TV ad with an explicitly linked radio or print/display ad can create similar or even enhanced processing outcomes that can substitute for additional TV ad exposures.

TAKEAWAYS

- Marketers must remember that successful communications require tapping into the right encoding processes (how information gets into memory) and retrieval processes (how information gets out of memory).

- To strengthen brand links, marketers sometimes try to make the brand name and package information more prominent in the ad. Although consumers may be better able to recall the advertised brand, it may also mean that fewer communication effects are created so that there is less other information about the brand to actually recall.

- Three cost-effective strategies to leverage already-created communication effects are brand signatures, advertising retrieval cues and coordinated media.

REFERENCES

Edell, Julie A. and Kevin Lane Keller (1989), "The Information Processing of Coordinated Media Campaigns," *Journal of Marketing Research*, 26 (May), 149–163.

Lane Keller, Kevin (2013), *Strategic Brand Management*, 4th ed., Upper Saddle River, NJ: Pearson Prentice-Hall.

Lane Keller, Kevin (1987), "Memory Factors in Advertising: The Effect of Advertising Retrieval Cues on Brand Evaluations," *Journal of Consumer Research*, 14 (December), 316–333.

Lane Keller, Kevin, Susan Heckler, and Michael J. Houston (1998), "The Effects of Brand Name Suggestiveness on Advertising Recall," *Journal of Marketing*, 62 (January), 48–57.

ENTRY #17

How can marketers foster brand attachment?

Andreas Eisingerich
Professor of Marketing, Imperial College, UK

Deborah J. MacInnis
Professor of Marketing, Marshall School of Business, University of Southern California

C. Whan Park
Professor of Marketing, Marshall School of Business, University of Southern California

What state characterizes a committed partnership? We use the term "brand attachment" to describe the psychological state underlying a brand relationship characterized as a committed partnership. We define brand attachment as the strength and prominence of the bond connecting the brand with the self. What this means is that consumers are committed to brands that strongly resonate with their goals, values, perspectives, and identities, and these brands are salient and top of mind.

How does this construct relate to a brand's equity? When consumers are strongly attached to a brand they not only have positive and strongly held attitudes toward it, they feel distress at the thought of the brand's unavailability in the marketplace, and they mourn the loss of such brands when they are discontinued. Moreover, enhancing consumers' brand attachment offers strong equity-building benefits to the firm. As brand attachment grows, consumers exhibit strong brand loyalty and brand advocacy behaviors; behaviors that maximize revenues while also reducing marketing costs. Brand loyalty behaviors include not just repeated brand purchase but also a willingness to pay a price premium, an unwillingness to substitute the brand for a different one when the favorite brand is not available, and a willingness to forgive a brand when it makes a mistake. Brand advocacy behaviors include recommending a brand to others, defending a brand when attacked, public showcasing of a brand, and active brand community involvement.

What induces this powerful state? Our most recent work finds that three psychological relationship-based factors underlie the state of brand attachment. These same factors underlie the strength of and commitment of a person to other people: trust, love and respect. The lack of any one factor strongly dilutes the strength of the brand relationship. While brand trust, love and respect individually affect brand attachment strength, they also interact in their effect on brand attachment strength. That is, each factor synergistically augments the effects of the other two in driving brand attachment.

While a number of brand actions can foster brand trust, love and respect, we find that the benefits that brands deliver strongly contribute to these states (and brand attachment). Specifically, a brand must offer functional (problem-solving) solutions that enable customers to make their lives easier and more convenient. These solutions that reliably and consistently do so become trusted. It also must offer experientially pleasing benefits that gratify customers. Brands that do so become loved. Moreover, a brand must stand for inspiring and self-enhancing values or principles, which, in turn, leads to brand respect.

TAKEAWAYS

- Stronger brand attachment induces greater loyalty and advocacy behaviors from consumers; behaviors which enhance brand equity and brand longevity in competitive markets.

- Consumers become most attached to brands that they trust, love, and respect.

- A brand's functionally empowering benefits, experientially gratifying benefits and symbolically self-enhancing benefits enhance brand trust, love and respect and hence strengthen brand attachment.

- When they are attached to brands, buying competitive brands creates a state of psychological discomfort for consumers.

REFERENCES

Park, C. Whan, Deborah J. MacInnis, Joseph Priester, Andreas Eisingerich, and Dawn Iacobucci (2010), "Brand Attachment and Strong Positive Brand Attitudes: Conceptual and Empirical Differentiation of Two Critical Brand Equity Drivers," *Journal of Marketing*, 74 (November), 1–17.

Park, C. Whan, Joseph W. Priester, and Deborah J. MacInnis (2009), "Brand Attachment: Construct, Consequences, and Causes", *Foundations and Trends in Marketing*, 1 (3), 191–230.

Park, C. W., Deborah J. MacInnis, and Andreas Eisingerich (2016), *Brand Admiration: Building a Business that People Love*, New York: Wiley.

ENTRY #18

When does your positional advantage pose challenges to success?

Rebecca J. Slotegraaf

Professor of Marketing and Whirlpool Faculty Fellow, Kelley School of Business, Indiana University

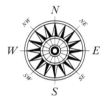

Innovation is essential for firm success, and to enhance success, firms endeavor to introduce numerous new products. Yet, new product failure rates remain high. When launching new products, firms and their brands encounter various hurdles toward achieving success as they face an increasingly competitive marketplace and strive to live up to consumer desires, needs and expectations.

One critical factor that we know helps drive new product success is the dedication of sufficient resources across the innovation process. However, if each firm within the same industry, or each brand within the same category, were to dedicate the same level of resources toward their new products, would we expect the products to attain similar degrees of success? The answer is no.

One might expect brands with higher equity to have an advantage when launching new products, and therefore attain higher success. Indeed, higher equity brands have already established awareness, familiarity and strong, positive associations, which often enables them to gain higher immediate returns from their marketing-mix efforts relative to their lower-equity rivals. Yet, when it comes to new product introductions, our research underscores certain barriers that can impede higher equity brands.

New product introductions tend to signal something new to the market, which generates attention. However, this new attention generates greater benefits for lower equity brands than for higher equity brands that have already established awareness. Higher equity brands are also likely to face certain pitfalls, such as cannibalization and potential brand dilution, from new product introductions. In our research, we show that the introduction of new products is an avenue through which lower equity brands may realize greater long-term sales effects from marketing promotions.

In addition, as firms search for ways to respond to new consumer trends, managers of higher equity brands need to be cognizant of the strong associations that they have established. Our research on one particular consumer trend highlights this issue for new product introductions. With a global push toward environmental sustainability, firms are increasingly introducing environmentally sustainable, or "green", new products as a response of this trend. Our research shows that the associations the brand and its parent firm have established limit the value gained from launching green new products. In particular, if a firm's environmental footprint has not established a favorable impression, it is challenging to change consumers' brand attitudes merely by introducing green new products. Similarly, considering the well-entrenched attitudes associated for older brands, they tend to face the same challenges.

In general, stronger brands are able to provide a basic set of advantages that a manager can leverage to strive for a competitive advantage. Yet, this base can also produce challenges when the brand engages in new product introduction efforts.

TAKEAWAYS

- Do not assume that higher equity brands are always in a favorable position when launching new products.

- Delineate the aspects that build a brand's equity, so that each can be dissected to understand whether challenges will occur for new product introduction efforts.

- Be careful to understand that smaller or lower equity brands may be at an advantage when the market sees a shift in consumer trends.

REFERENCES

Olsen, Mitchell C., Rebecca J. Slotegraaf, and Sandeep R. Chandukala (2014), "Green Claims and Message Frames: How Green New Products Change Brand Attitude," *Journal of Marketing*, 78 (5), 119–137.

Slotegraaf, Rebecca J. (2012), "Keep the Door Open: Innovating Toward a More Sustainable Future," *Journal of Product Innovation Management*, 29 (3), 349–351.

Slotegraaf, Rebecca J. and Koen Pauwels (2008), "The Impact of Brand Equity and Innovation on the Long-term Effectiveness of Promotions," *Journal of Marketing Research*, 45 (3), 293–306.

ENTRY #19

How does your advertising affect consumers?

Charles R. Taylor

John A. Murphy Professor of Marketing, Villanova School of Business

From the beginning of my career, I have enjoyed work that has managerial and/or societal implications. While I started out as a generalist, I gradually gravitated toward topics that have something to with advertising—and international advertising, advertising effects, or regulatory or societal issues were my most common areas of inquiry.

My international work has focused on the degree to which cultural factors force modifications to advertising. From the time I first studied this topic (1990) until approximately 30 years later, there was a focus on the idea of a debate on standardization versus local adaptation. Reading the introductory sections of studies, one would think that half of the field thought all marketing mix elements could be standardized while the other half thought nothing could be standardized. I always found this characterization puzzling as my own research, and that of many others, painted a very different picture. Studies were consistently finding that in markets that had certain similarities (e.g., economic development, competition) standardization of broader strategic aspects of an ad such as main selling proposition, positioning, and central theme led to more effective cross-national campaigns. Executional variables, however, such as commercial format, settings, story type, etc., usually needed to be adapted. I wrote an article for the *Journal of Advertising* that I hope helped to point this out. The last decade has seen significant advances in understanding cross-cultural advertising, thanks largely to more focus on consumer culture theory rather than a false "debate."

My research on advertising portrayals of Asian Americans has also received a good bit of attention. What I hope this stream of research demonstrated is the idea that expectancy theory and cultivation theory suggest that even portrayals of "positive" stereotypes can be problematic. Thus, when Asian-Americans are highly over-represented in ads for technical products and in workplace settings and business relationships (as opposed to settings or relationships involving family and friends), this reinforces a "model minority" stereotype that does not capture Asian Americans as individuals. Such subtle stereotypes can operate to put pressure on children in Asian American communities and the reality is that these children report higher incidence of self-esteem and anxiety issues. Hopefully, greater awareness of the potential impact of such portrayals can help the situation.

Finally, the work I have done on advertising and public policy issues has been rewarding. My studies on outdoor advertising and how it works, rooted in selective perception and retail gravity models, along with work on the benefits it provides to smaller, more local advertisers have been rewarding in that it has made a difference in policy debates. Similarly, work I have done on controversial issues such as alcohol advertising, tobacco advertising, on premise sign issues and green marketing has had policy implications that has gotten noticed, often in court cases and via testimony to the U.S. Congress and State Legislatures. It is especially rewarding when the industry notices and a tribute to those in the marketing community who blazed the trail on public policy and marketing.

TAKEAWAYS

- Standardize strategy and adapt executions in global advertising.

- Advertising portrayals reinforcing subtle stereotypes can be harmful.

- Minority groups should be portrayed in a variety of contexts.

- Academic research on marketing and public policy issues really matters!

REFERENCES

Capella, Michael L., Charles R. Taylor, and Jeremy Kees (2012), "Tobacco Harm Reduction Advertising in the Presence of a Government Mandated Warning," *Journal of Consumer Affairs*, 46 (2), 235–259.

Ford, John B., Barbara Mueller, and Charles R. Taylor (2011), "The Tension between Strategy and Execution: Challenges for International Advertising Research," *Journal of Advertising Research*, 51 (1), 27–41.

Okazaki, Shintaro, Charles R. Taylor, and Shaoming Zou (2006), "Advertising Standardization's Positive Impact on the Bottom Line: A Model of When and How Standardization Improves Financial and Strategic Performance," *Journal of Advertising*, 35 (Fall), 17–33.

Rotfeld, Herbert J. and Charles R. Taylor (2009), "The Advertising Regulation and Self-Regulation Issues Ripped from the Headlines with (Sometimes Missed) Opportunities for Disciplined Multi-disciplinary Research," *Journal of Advertising*, 38 (4), 5–14.

Taylor, Charles R., Stacy Landreth, and Hae-Kyong Bang (2005), "Asian Americans in Magazine Advertising: Portrayals of the 'Model Minority,'" *Journal of Macromarketing*, 25 (2), 153–162.

Taylor, Charles R. and Ju Yung Lee (1994), "Not in Vogue: Portrayals of Asian Americans in Magazine Advertising." *Journal of Public Policy & Marketing*, 13 (2), 239–245.

Taylor, Charles R. and Shintaro Okazaki (2015), "Do Global Brands Use Similar Executional Styles Across Cultures? A Comparison of U.S. and Japanese Television Advertising," *Journal of Advertising*, 44 (3), 276–288.

Taylor, Charles R. and Matthew Sarkees (2016), "Do Bans on Illuminated On-Premise Signs Matter? Balancing Environmental Impact with the Impact on Businesses," *International Journal of Advertising*, 35 (1), 61–73.

Taylor, Charles R. and Barbara B. Stern (1997), "Asian-Americans: Television Advertising and the 'Model Minority' Stereotype," *Journal of Advertising*, 26 (2), 1–15.

Taylor, Charles R., R. Dale Wilson, and Gordon E. Miracle (1997), "The Impact of Information Level Strategies on the Effectiveness of Korean Vs. U.S. Television Commercials," *Journal of Advertising*, 26 (1), 1–18.

ENTRY #20

How can you use your brand to help your consumers live better lives?

Deborah Roedder John

Curtis L. Carlson Chair in Marketing, Carlson School of Management, University of Minnesota

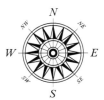

Many of us struggle to feel more positive about ourselves, wishing we were younger-looking, more glamorous, or athletic. We also struggle at times with challenging tasks in our lives, whether it is finishing an important work project, getting through a tough exercise routine, or just trying to get our child to eat vegetables.

A large industry has emerged to help us with these issues. Self-help books, new age diet plans, personal trainers, fashion stylists, and life coaches offer the promise of helping us to live better lives.

But, our research points to something else that should be added to the list—brands. We have found that using brands can make us feel more attractive, more intelligent, and more confident about our abilities. And, the benefits do not stop with feelings. Brands can help us perform better on challenging tasks, whether that happens to be completing a tough workout or answering math questions on a GRE exam.

Can this really be true? Let us take a look at some of the evidence. In one of our studies, we asked participants to exercise with a handgrip while drinking tap water from a plain plastic cup or the same cup with a Gatorade sticker. Gatorade is a brand known for promising better athletic performance. We found that participants who drank from the Gatorade cup were able to squeeze the handgrip more times during the exercise period than participants drinking from the plain cup.

Not convinced? Let us take a look at another study. We asked a group of undergraduate students to take a sample GRE exam, with difficult math questions, and gave them a pen to record their answers. One group used a pen engraved with the MIT name and logo, while a second group used a plain pen. Of course, there is nothing about an MIT pen that imbues someone with skills to answer tough math questions. But, students who used the MIT pen answered more of the difficult math questions correctly.

What is happening here? In both cases, the brand made our participants feel more confident about their ability to complete the handgrip exercise or answer the tough math questions. It is what psychologists call self-efficacy, which motivates us to be persistent and to work through difficulties we have completing really challenging tasks.

Does the beneficial effect of brands work for everyone? Our research shows that it tends to be most evident for certain types of individuals. Our studies show that people who have fixed mindsets (entity theorists), who believe they cannot improve their skills through efforts at self-improvement, have the most to gain from using brands as we describe. On the other hand, people who have growth mindsets (incremental theorists), who believe they can increase their skills through their own efforts at self-improvement, show little gain from using the same brands.

TAKEAWAYS

- Brands are marketing tools, but they can also be an important positive force in our lives.

- Certain individuals benefit more from using brands. If you feel your abilities are fixed in a certain area (e.g., "I am not athletic"), you can benefit from using a brand associated with athletic performance.

REFERENCES

Park, Ji Kyung and Deborah Roedder John (2010), "Got to Get You into My Life: Do Brand Personalities Rub Off on Consumers?" *Journal of Consumer Research*, 37 (December), 655–669.

Park, Ji Kyung and Deborah Roedder John (2014), "I Think I Can, I Think I Can: Brand Use, Self-Efficacy, and Performance," *Journal of Marketing Research*, 51 (April), 233–247.

John, Deborah Roedder and Ji Kyung Park (2016), "Mindsets Matter: Implications for Branding Research and Practice," *Journal of Consumer Psychology*, 26 (January), 153–160.

ENTRY #21

Why hire someone who does not fit consumers' stereotypes?

Valerie S. Folks

Robert E. Brooker Chair and Professor of Marketing, Marshall School of Business, University of Southern California

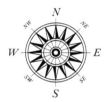

What are your stereotypes about the typical physician, nurse, chef, or professor? People share stereotypes about many occupations, such as notions about the kind of person who is the typical financial services advisor, and about the kind of person who is the typical wedding planner. Those stereotypes often incorporate basic ways we categorize people, such as whether a person is a man or a woman, or is young or old.

How do such stereotypes influence consumers' judgments? Does the service provider who fits a customer's stereotypes about that occupation have an edge over one who does not in terms of creating a better impression on customers? For example, do customers assume more or less ability from a female financial planner given that the stereotypical advisor is a man, or, conversely assume more or less ability from a male wedding planner given that the stereotypical planner is a woman? And do those inferences about a counter stereotypical employee influence beliefs about the company as a whole?

Our research shows that consumers react differently to a counter stereotypical person and these different reactions can benefit the firm under certain circumstances. People make more extreme judgments about a counter stereotypical service provider's ability, inferring that the person is either much less able or much more able than a stereotypical provider. Beliefs in someone's ability and competence are important because they lead to confidence in one's expectations for future job performance. For example, a consumer's belief that an excellent piece of advice from a woman financial planner is due to her ability leads the consumer to be confident in getting continued excellent advice from her.

Whether consumers infer better or worse ability depends on how much and what kind of evidence there is. When the evidence is meager, is mixed, or implies mediocre performance, the counter stereotypical person is judged less able than a stereotypical person. For example, a mediocre piece of advice from a woman financial planner leads to inferences that she is less able and competent at her job compared to the same advice from a man. In contrast, evidence of superior job performance leads the counter stereotypical person to be judged more able and competent than the stereotypical person.

Further, beliefs that the counter stereotypical person is more able impact inferences about the firm more generally. Consumers assume that not only is the counter stereotypical person different from and more able than others in that same profession, but also that the employee's company is different from and superior to its competitors. For example, consumers believe that a woman who performs well as a financial advisor is more able and more competent as compared to a man who performs the same way. They also infer that her firm is superior to other financial planning firms. This is a useful finding for marketers because we are always searching for ways to distinguish our brand in consumers' minds.

How powerful are these effects? Stereotypes are so powerful that they can color a consumer's firsthand product experience. For example, those who listened to a competent woman conductor's powerful music described her music in more complex ways, as having powerful as well as delicate aspects, which differentiated her performance from when listeners knew nothing about the conductor's gender or when the conductor was described as a man. Listeners had a more singular experience from a counter stereotypical performer.

TAKEAWAYS

- There is a potential upside, in terms of consumers' judgments, when a firm employs a counter stereotypical person to deliver service or create products.

- Employees, if you do not fit the stereotype for your profession, be aware that you may have to go to more lengths to prove competence, but that being different can help you and your organization stand out.

- Customers, if your service provider is not the stereotypical person you expect, be open-minded. Your stereotypes may bias your judgments.

REFERENCES

Folkes, Valerie and Shashi Matta (2013), "When a Product Takes on Characteristics of the Person Who Created It: Sometimes It Sounds Sweeter," *Journal of Consumer Psychology*, 23 (1), 19–35.

Matta, Shashi and Valerie Folkes (2005), "Inferences about Firms from Counter-Stereotypical Service Providers," *Journal of Consumer Research*, 32 (September), 196–206.

DESTINATION #4

Enhancing the marketplace

ENTRY #22

Price competition, attraction effects, and line-extension effects: What are their hidden returns?

Timothy B. Heath

Professor, Muma College of Business, University of South Florida

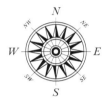

Three asymmetries reveal hidden returns to quality best appreciated by first understanding dominance: A dominates B if A is superior to B on at least one dimension (e.g., quality) and inferior on none (e.g., price). Example: when A offers more quality than B while charging the same price, meaning there is no price-quality trade-off and essentially no one chooses (the dominated) Brand B.

1. Asymmetric Price Competition. Various studies find that discounting a higher-quality (HQ) brand's price attracts more consumers from a lower-quality (LQ) brand than discounting an LQ brand's price attracts from an HQ brand. At least two benefits from improving disadvantages (e.g., HQ's price) contribute: (1) improving on the dimension more important to our competitor's customers, and (2) enabling dominance over our competitor. Imagine an orange juice brand, HQ, which charges $3.34 and offers 66/80 quality, and its competitor, LQ, which charges $2.99 and offers 56/80 quality. If HQ discounts price, the dimension more important to LQ's customers, to $2.99, it dominates LQ by offering more quality while charging the same price. LQ, however,

cannot dominate HQ by reducing its price even to $0.00 because the price/quality trade-off remains and HQ consumers may still (rationally) prefer HQ. When trade-offs exist across competitors, dominance can be produced only by improving and erasing disadvantages, the dimensions valued most by our competitors' customers, and price discounts tend to pull consumers up in quality more than down.

2. Asymmetric Attraction Effects. Numerous studies show that if we add (to the brands above) a third brand (MQ) at 61 quality and $3.34 price (HQ's price), it will increase HQ's share and reduce LQ's share because HQ but not LQ dominates MQ (i.e., HQ's objective superiority over MQ increases HQ's appeal). Our meta-analysis of attraction effects found that most arose primarily when the target (dominating) brand was at higher quality but not when it was at lower quality, meaning in our example that LQ would benefit relatively little if we added an LQ2 brand at 56 quality and $3.19 price. Consumers are again moved to higher quality more easily than lower quality (though this general effect did reverse in a more impoverished area).

3. Asymmetric Line-Extension Effects. Imagine that we have a middle-quality brand such as Foster's beer and add a moderately higher-quality line extension (HQE; Fosters Select) or lower-quality line extension (LQE; e.g., Fosters Grog). Across a number of brands and product classes, we find that HQEs improve overall brand eva-luation significantly more than LQEs damage it, the latter effect often being minimal. The asymmetry arises largely because consumers see HQE's as more relevant to brand evaluation than LQEs, with HQEs considered positive and LQEs neutral. HQE's also improve perceived brand expertise, innovativeness, and prestige more than LQEs damage them.

TAKEAWAYS

- If you can enter a market above or below a single competitor on price/quality levels, consider entering above them. Your short-term price reductions should then maximize share thefts by improving on the dimension valued most by your competitor's customers, and the dimension able to produce dominance over your competitor if improved sufficiently (i.e., to at or beyond your competitor's level). Caveat: Were all competitors to improve on their disadvantages simultaneously (e.g., HQ reducing price permanently and LQ improving quality), they would race toward commoditization (no differentiation) and the harsh price competition and meager profits it would bring (i.e., avoid a disadvantages war if possible).

- Beware competitors entering above you in price/quality or improving on their disadvantages. If competitors focus on improving disadvantages, you should consider quickly invading their territory by improving on your own disadvantages/their advantages (game theory's tit-for-tat rule). If they back down from a disadvantages war, however, you may want to do the same and improve on a mix of advantages and disadvantages to maintain differentiation while discouraging market entrants (improving on only advantages would increase differentiation but also produce extreme cross-brand differences that may invite entrants).

- Adding a moderately higher-quality product to your brand's line should improve overall brand evaluation and let you dominate your own products through short-term price discounts should that appear profitable. Example: The Economist once offered $59 online, $125 print, and $125 online-plus-print subscriptions, such that the combination's dominance over the print subscription no doubt increased the combination's sales (which could also have been achieved by pricing the combination at $175 and then discounting it to $125). Caveat: Beware of offering line extensions too far above your current brand's quality image lest your extension exceed its conceptual grasp (e.g., the Volkswagen Phaeton's failure in the U.S.).

REFERENCES

Heath, Timothy B. and Subimal Chatterjee (1995), "Asymmetric Decoy Effects on Lower Quality and Higher-Quality Brands: Meta-Analytic and Experimental Evidence," *Journal of Consumer Research*, 22 (December), 268–284.

Heath, Timothy B., Devon DelVecchio, and Michael S. McCarthy (2011), "The Asymmetric Effects of Extending Brands to Lower and Higher Quality," *Journal of Marketing*, 75 (July), 3–20.

Heath, Timothy B., Gangseog Ryu, Subimal Chatterjee, Michael S. McCarthy, David L. Mothersbaugh, Sandra J. Milberg, and Gary J. Gaeth (2000), "Asymmetric Competition in Choice and the Leveraging of Competitive Disadvantages," *Journal of Consumer Research*, 27 (December), 291–308.

ENTRY #23

What makes a new product successful?

Donald R. Lehmann

George E. Warren Professor of Business, Columbia Business School

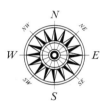

It is easy to identify successful new products after they have succeeded. It is considerably harder to do so before they hit the market. Nonetheless, several factors can help predict success or failure.

1. **The idea itself**
   Generally speaking, ideas derived from providing solutions to problems customers have (active wants) have a better chance to succeed as do those from observing an (often crude) solution to a problem someone has developed/cobbled together. On the other hand, "mental inventions" dreamed up by individuals removed from contact with actual customers and attempts to follow trends which have already "left the station" are likely to fail (i.e., the tenth version is not "cool").

2. **The new benefit the innovator offers**
   (It is the product, stupid) Innovations which provide a clear (and easy to observe) advantage on a relevant aspect (a better mousetrap) have a better chance to succeed. By contrast, innovations which ask customers to change (are not compatible with) their current behavior patterns or to take on risks (operating, social, psychological, or financial) are met with resistance.

3. **The right amount of different**
   New ideas that are not very new ("lemon-scented" new products) have limited potential. On the other hand, major innovations are

difficult for customers to categorize and can be "too new" which means at a minimum it would take a long time and substantial effort to get people to buy them.

4. **Whether the company's reputation (brand) has "permission" to sell products**
   Many failures (BenGay aspirin, Levi's suites) involve extensions to categories that do not match a company's image or perceived competence even if the products are good ones. Establishing a broad brand image or convincing customers a new product fits the current image is an important step toward success.

5. **Catchiness**
   In an increasing socially connected world, the influence of other customers often swamps marketing effort. This makes the behavior of key individuals (variously known as influential, opinion leaders, and hubs) and their willingness to advocate the innovation to others important. It also means that successful innovations tend to create dense geographic or social network adoption patterns. This makes the ability to encourage contagion quite important (interestingly the mathematical models of new product adoption are the same ones used by the Centers for Disease Control to model the spread of diseases). Pragmatically, grabbing a substantial (20%) share of the eventual market early is important for long-term success.

6. **Stickiness**
   Customers tend to resist giving up products they value. They also purchase add-ons (e.g., for a car, extended warrantees, rust proofing, and numerous dealer installed options)

7. **Breathing space**
   Competition rarely allows an innovation to be in a market by itself for long. Its absence, or at least delay in it responding, is a major advantage.

8. **The support behind it**
   Effort is required to generate awareness and interest. Information is typically needed to allow potential customers to evaluate new products, and means offered to have easy access to the product (e.g. via channels customers use). Put differently, "standard" marketing matters and firms need to be able to produce, finance, market and manage a new product to make it successful.

None of these eight factors alone—or in combination—guarantee success but they all improve the odds for it.

TAKEAWAYS

- When gauging a product's potential success, it is important to:

  - Assess the product itself, new benefits it offers, and its differentiating factors
  - Determine whether the product is in line with the company's brand and overall image

- Ask important questions, such as:

  - Will the product catch on?
  - Is this product sticky?
  - Will this product have breathing space?
  - Will the product be supported?

REFERENCES

Garber, Tal, Jacob Goldenberg, Barak Libai, and Eitan Muller (2014), "From Density to Destiny: Using Spatial Dimension of Sales Data for Early Prediction of New Product Success," *Marketing Science*, 23 (Summer), 419–428.

Goldenberg, Jacob, Donald R. Lehmann, and David Mazursky (2001), "The Idea Itself and the Circumstances of Its Emergence as Predictors of New Product Success," *Management Science*, 47 (January), 69–84.

Holak, Susan L. and Donald R. Lehmann (1990), "Purchase Intentions and the Dimensions of Innovation: An Exploratory Model," *Journal of Product Innovation Management*, 7 (March), 59–73.

Parker, Jeffrey R., Donald R. Lehmann, Kevin Lane Keller, and Martin G. Schleicher (2018), "Building a Multi-Category Brand: When Should Distant Brand Extensions Be Introduced," *Journal of the Academy of Marketing Science*, 2.

Rogers, Everett M. (2003), *Diffusion of Innovation*, New York: Free Press.

ENTRY #24

What are the consequences for remedying risk?

Lisa E. Bolton

Professor of Marketing, Smeal College of Business,
The Pennsylvania State University

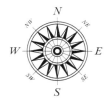

Risk is present in a variety of everyday consumption experiences: for example, eating ice cream, smoking, and driving all pose risks for consumer health and safety. Consumption also poses societal risks: for example, consumer decisions regarding energy usage and trash disposal pose environmental risks. And, of course, consumers face financial risks with consumption, as evidenced by credit card (mis)use and debt.

Consumer welfare advocates often promote risk avoidance to help consumers deal with risk: "just say no" campaigns, smoking cessation programs, and cutting up credit cards are examples. However, remedy marketing offers an alternative to risk avoidance. Remedies refer to products or services designed to mitigate risk—and these offerings provide a way for consumers to manage risk in their everyday lives. Unfortunately, remedies can sometimes "boomerang"—by taking the risk out of risky behavior, remedies may inadvertently encourage it, especially among those most at risk. (For example, messages about smoking cessation aids undermines risk perceptions and quitting intentions among smokers.) The appeal of remedies is self-evident: why live a healthy (financially responsible) lifestyle when a drug (debt consolidation loan) can take care of the problem? The boomerang emerges with exposure to remedy marketing and in response to remedy consumption itself. For example, consumers make less healthy food decisions after consuming a functional food and make less environmentally responsible decisions after choosing an eco-product.

The net effect of remedies in terms of risk will depend upon many factors. Remedies that offer little in the way of risk-reduction (e.g., heart-healthy chocolate?) may net negative due to the boomerang, and even remedies that reduce specific risks (e.g., cholesterol drugs) could expose consumers to other risks (e.g., of a sedentary lifestyle). Happily, there are ways to address the boomerang—but informational interventions can be effortful. (To illustrate: If you give me nine minutes with every consumer in America, I have a video to help them understand debt consolidation!) Simpler nudges may provide a more feasible solution. For example, eco-products do not boomerang when consumers are nudged toward consistency in environmental responsibility.

What intrigues me in the phenomena that I have studied is how remedy marketing serves as a unique impetus that triggers the boomerang. (Close cousins to my work include risk compensation and licensing.) Because firms tend to promote remedies, their marketing budgets will swamp the more modest efforts to promote risk avoidance by consumer welfare advocates. Hence, the marketplace playing field tilts toward managing risk rather than avoiding it. Likewise, consumer biases like motivated reasoning may also favour managing risk via remedies rather than avoiding it. After all, who does not want to have their cake and eat it too? (And, if the cake has omega-3s, I will have another slice!)

At a broader level, the boomerang could account for why innovation sometimes fails to solve societal problems. For example, obesity continues to rise despite the proliferation of functional foods promoting health benefits, and environmental harm continues despite innovations that deliver environmental benefits. The reluctance of consumers to adopt such innovations is often cited as a driver of societal problems. If only consumers would purchase energy-efficient light bulbs and eat low-fat products! However, "innovating our way out" of problems, both at the individual and societal level, may be more difficult than we realize—especially when remedies boomerang on the very risks they seek to manage.

TAKEAWAYS

- Do not assume that remedies, products or services that mitigate risk will do so.
- Assess the impact of remedies on immediate and downstream behavior, as well as complementary protective behavior (such as risk avoidance).
- Incorporate interventions and nudges to mitigate the boomerang of remedy marketing.

REFERENCES

Bhattacharjee, Amit, Lisa E. Bolton, and Americus Reed II (2015), "The Perils of Marketing Weight Management Remedies and the Role of Health Literacy," *Journal of Public Policy & Marketing*, 34 (Spring), 50–62.

Bolton, Lisa E., Paul N. Bloom, and Joel B. Cohen (2011), "Facts about Debt Consolidation Loans", a financial literacy video available to consumers and financial advisors. Funded by the National Endowment for Financial Education. Available at: www.nefe.org/what-we-provide/primary-research/debt-consolidation-loan-research.aspx

Bolton, Lisa E., Paul N. Bloom, and Joel B. Cohen (2011), "Using Loan Plus Lender Literacy Information to Combat One-sided Marketing of Debt Consolidation Loans," *Journal of Marketing Research*, 48 (special issue), S51–S59. Funded by the National Endowment for Financial Education and a Smeal Research Grant.

Bolton, Lisa E., Joel B. Cohen, and Paul N. Bloom (2006), "Does Marketing Products as Remedies Create 'Get Out of Jail Free Cards'?" *Journal of Consumer Research*, 33 (June), 71–81.

Bolton, Lisa E., Americus Reed II, Kevin G. Volpp, and Katrina Armstrong (2008), "How Does Drug and Supplement Marketing Affect a Healthy Lifestyle?" *Journal of Consumer Research*, 34 (May), 713–726.

Garvey, Aaron M. and Lisa E. Bolton (2016), "The Licensing Effect Revisited: How Virtuous Behavior Heightens the Pleasure Derived from Subsequent Hedonic Consumption," *Journal of Marketing Behavior*, 2 (April), 291–298.

Garvey, Aaron and Lisa E. Bolton (2017), "Eco-Product Choice Cuts Both Ways: How Pro-Environmental Licensing versus Reinforcement is Contingent upon Environmental Consciousness," *Journal of Public Policy & Marketing*, 36 (2), 284–298.

Wang, Wenbo, Hean Tat Keh, and Lisa E. Bolton (2010), "Lay Theories of Medicine and a Healthy Lifestyle," *Journal of Consumer Research*, 37 (June), 80–97.

ENTRY #25

Why do business relationships often fail and how can you turn that trend around?

Sandy D. Jap

Sarah Beth Brown Endowed Professor of Marketing, Goizueta Business School, Emory University

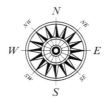

For the past 20 years, I have studied relationships, partnerships, and alliances. I wanted to understand how to expand the pie of benefits for both parties. Instead, I found that relationships tend to fail, more than they succeed. The reasons, found across various disciplines, underscore aspects of relationship development and management that make them prone to "the dark side." The reasons are outlined in my recent book, *Partnering with the Frenemy*, but here are some of the most common:

1. Trust is more easily lost than built—many make the mistake of thinking of trust like a bank account—deposits grow the balance and withdrawals reduce it. A more appropriate metaphor is to think of trust as water levels in a bathtub—it builds slowly, but is quick to drain. Trust is built in regular gestures (flows) over time, but can be easily lost, even on the basis of suspicions. Once lost, it takes time to rebuild.
2. Grand gestures make things worse—continuing with the bathtub metaphor, the best way to fill it is to let the water levels rise continually in a steady state, instead of dumping massive amounts into it at one time. The same is true with relationships—grand

gestures exceed expectations and make them worse. Like the spouse who receives flowers from a partner who hates giving flowers (a grand gesture meant to have a big improvement on the relationship), the relationship suffers and leaves the recipient suspicious, instead of more appreciative.

3. A bad history poisons today—relationships that develop in a healthy manner—through periods of joint exploration, build-up, and maturity fare better than those that require restarting, rebuilding, or move toward commitment too quickly. Parties do not easily forgive and forget, nor do they move on to rebuild in a more constructive manner. A bad history colors their evaluations of performance, and stubbornly so.

Thus, I implore mangers to realize that trust takes time to build and how you build, matters. Pie expansion does not happen with a rush to long-term commitments or the investments of a single party. Open and frequent communication is critical—it is better to speak up about what bothers you than to let it go. Both partners need to be aware of their alternatives, and be willing to move on when the value is no longer there. Lose the marriage metaphor and think of business as being more like dating, since ending the latter is not as painful and stigmatizing as a divorce. In other words, learn to say goodbye nicely. Mutual customers and stakeholders must be considered and thorough communication at multiple levels of the organization is critical.

Finally, partnering only makes sense if value creation involves customization or tacit know-how. Differentiated partners, few alternatives and fast-moving industries with fluctuating demand are also conducive. If there is a golden bullet, it would be that dedicated, investments from both sides make pie-expansion work. Specialized equipment, dedicated personnel, organizational processes and foregone opportunities are key to sustaining commitment over time.

TAKEAWAYS

- Trust is more easily lost than built.
- Grand gestures make things worse.
- A bad history poisons today.
- Learn to say goodbye nicely.
- Dedicated investments from both sides make pie-expansion work.

Turning the failing trend around

REFERENCES

Anderson, E. and Sandy D. Jap (2005), "The Dark-Side of Close Relationships," *Sloan Management Review*, 46 (3), 75–82.

Dalsace, Frédéric, and Sandy D. Jap (2017), "The Friend or Foe Fallacy, or Why Your Best Customers Don't Need Your Friendship," *Business Horizons*, 60 (4), 483–493.

Jap, Sandy D. (2016), *Partnering with the Frenemy*, London: Pearson FT Press.

Jap, Sandy D. and Erin Anderson (2007), "Testing a Life-Cycle Theory of Cooperative Interorganizational Relationships: Movement Across Stages and Performance," *Management Science*, 53 (2), 260–275.

Jap, Sandy D., Noel Gould, and Annie Liu (2017), "Managing Mergers: Why People First Can Improve Brand and IT Consolidations" *Business Horizons*, 60, 123–134.

Jap, Sandy D., Diana C. Robertson, and Ryan Hamilton (2011), "The Dark Side of Rapport: Agent Misbehavior Face-to-Face and Online," Special Issue on Marketing Within the Enterprise and Beyond, Pradeep Chintagunta and Preyas Desai (eds.), *Management Science*, 57 (9), 1610–1622.

Wang, Qiong, Ujwal Kayande, and Sandy D. Jap, (2010), "The Seeds of Dissolution: Discrepancy and Incoherence in Buyer-Supplier Exchange," *Marketing Science*, 29 (6), 1109–1124.

ENTRY #26

Is it better for us (and our consumers) to make decisions together or alone?

Cait Lamberton

Ben L. Fryrear Chair and Associate Professor in Marketing, Katz Graduate School of Business, University of Pittsburgh

We know why a focus on individual choice is so prevalent in marketing. It is easy and clean. But how many decisions do we really make in this kind of isolation? When are our decisions actually independent of the obligations we feel to others?

Increasingly, it is clear that psychological health is, in part, determined by our ability to both decide alone and decide together, and to shift across these capacities dynamically over the course of our lives. Sometimes, deciding alone can be important, because we each have unique sets of tools and traits from which to draw—and compromise can be detrimental. But sometimes, deciding-with can lead to better outcomes.

The trick is learning when to do which, and this raises the second big lesson: surrounding yourself with people whose decisions elevate rather than detract is absolutely critical. Working with Hristina Nikolova at Boston College, we have learned that couples that include two low self-control individuals will tend to indulge at about the same rate when they decide together as opposed to alone, and couples where both partners are paragons of restraint will restrict themselves the same way alone as together. But the far more common case is that couples include one low and one high self-control partner. You know this couple: there is a "fun and crazy" one and a "solid and careful" one, and the jokes that "opposites attract" have been flowing since the day they met.

But our research shows that this causes problems: the "solid and careful" partner will likely give into the "fun and crazy" partner's request to rent this slightly more expensive apartment, lease this pricier car, or order dessert—because old "solid and careful" tends to put their own immediate gratification aside for the good of the relationship. In short, "solid and careful" does not want to fight about it, so they give in against their better judgment. Over the long-term, this pattern can lead to debt, unhealthy lifestyles, and harm to the relationship.

On the other hand, there are also cases where deciding-with makes us the best version of ourselves. In studying ethical decision making, Hristina, Nicole Verrochi Coleman, and I find that whether deciding-with makes you more or less moral depends on how close you are to your decision making partner. Pairs of acquaintances are actually more likely to bend the rules than are individuals, because, let us face it, being bad together offers a bonding opportunity. But when we have known someone for a long time, the opposite happens: they hold us accountable. And that means that we are more ethical than we would be if deciding alone. Deciding-with, in that case, elevates us.

Calls to think beyond the individual and to focus on societal concerns are valid and extremely important. At the same time, I would argue that thinking beyond the individual not only offers us a better idea of what consumers will do, it helps us understand the path to our own growth and well-being.

TAKEAWAYS

- Do not assume that decision-making strategies observed when people make solo decisions will hold when consumers make decisions in pairs or couples.

- If predicting behavior based on personality, capture not only a given consumer's traits, but also the traits of people in their immediate social network.

- Make sure you understand consumers' interpersonal goals when they make decisions with others. Some interpersonal goals may override other choice criteria or social norms.

REFERENCES

Dzoghleva, Hristina and Cait Lamberton (2014), "Should Birds of a Feather Flock Together? Understanding Self-Control Decisions in Dyads," *Journal of Consumer Research*, 41 (2), 361–380.

Lamberton, Cait (2016), "Collaborative Consumption," *Current Opinion in Psychology*, 10, 55–59.

Nikolova, Hristina and Cait Lamberton (2016), "Men in the Middle: Male Decision Makers and the Compromise Effect," *Journal of Consumer Research*, 43 (3), 355–371.

Nikolova, Hristina, Cait Lamberton, and Nicole Verrochi Coleman (2018), "Stranger Danger: When and Why Consumer Dyads Behave Less Ethically Than Individuals," *Journal of Consumer Research*, (forthcoming).

ENTRY #27

What steps can you take to create an inclusive marketplace?

Sonya A. Grier
Professor of Marketing, American University

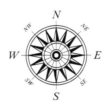

Marketplaces worldwide are challenged with how to manage growing racial, ethnic, and cultural diversity. Media fragmentation, family upbringing, and personal choices may limit consumer exposure to diverse cultures and worldviews. When people are ignorant of other social groups, they may become resistant to instead of accepting marketplace diversity. What is the role of marketing in exacerbating and ameliorating these challenges?

Consider the crossover of ethnic films, which expose people to images of lifestyles they may not ordinarily encounter. The movement from "niche" to "mainstream" markets often has implications for financial viability and social inclusion. Yet ethnic-oriented products are often targeted solely toward the referent ethnic group given concerns that other groups will be uninterested. Our research found that both black and white consumers were indeed more likely to attend movies featuring members of their own group. However, a moderating variable we added, based on our own self-referencing, showed robust effects: those who were more interested in other cultures were more interested in movies featuring other races.

We further developed this idea into a construct we call "diversity seeking" and define it as an individual's propensity to seek out products, services, and experiences of cultures different from their own. The diversity seeking scale identifies and encompasses two factors—a learning subscale that reflects one's tendency to explore other cultures via activities that allow experimentation and temporary interaction, and a living subscale that reflects a greater level of commitment to engage with diverse others.

Our scale development studies found that higher levels of diversity-seeking were associated with past diversity-related activities and a higher likelihood of engaging in future diversity-related behaviors. We also found that consumers high in diversity seeking were more likely to live in ethnically and culturally diverse areas, a finding that intrigued us regarding the relationship of the living and learning sub-scales. We explored these issues in the context of neighborhoods.

Increasing gentrification worldwide brings demographically diverse consumers into direct contact. This is notable, as in the United States, substantial segregation exists, and a wealth of research demonstrates the deleterious effects for consumers, such as differential access to educational, employment and social resources. Thus, sustaining integrated communities is an ongoing policy priority and significant to consumer researchers given the relationship to consumption and effects on consumer well-being.

We explored social and consumption dynamics among long-term and new residents in gentrifying neighborhoods. We found that new residents are often drawn to these neighborhoods based on a desire to live among diverse others. However, the increased neighborhood diversity did not lead to increased interaction between diverse residents. Rather, we observed tensions in the social and consumption domains that resulted in "faux-diversity" and a reduced sense-of-community.

Many research questions remain. At a broad level, how can we best leverage our understanding of diversity seekers to contribute to inclusive marketplaces? High diversity seeking consumers behave in ways that are inconsistent with conventional predictions of culture-consistent consumption behaviors. These "positive deviants" may lead us to strategies to develop sustainable diverse communities and support inclusive marketplaces worldwide.

TAKEAWAYS

- People who are interested in learning about and experiencing other cultures are not only potential targets for ethnic products, but also important "bridges" to motivate societal change.

- Marketplace diversity is not equivalent to marketplace inclusion.

- Neighborhoods are an important and relevant consumption context.

- Marketing efforts can identify strategies to create and support inclusive marketplaces.

REFERENCES

Brumbaugh, Anne M. and Sonya A. Grier (2013), "Agents of Change: A Scale to Identify Diversity Seekers," *Journal of Public Policy & Marketing*, 32, 144–155.

Grier, Sonya A. and Anne M. Brumbaugh (1999), "Noticing Cultural Differences: Advertising Meanings Created by Target and Non-Target Markets," *Journal of Advertising* 28 (1), 79–93.

Grier, Sonya A., Anne M. Brumbaugh, and Corliss G. Thornton (2006), "Crossover Dreams: Consumer Responses to Ethnic-Oriented Products," *Journal of Marketing*, 70 (2), 35–51.

Grier, Sonya A. and Vanessa G. Perry, "Dog Parks and Coffee Shops: Consumption and Faux-Diversity in Gentrifying Neighborhoods," *Journal of Public Policy & Marketing* (forthcoming).

Grier, Sonya A. and Vanessa G. Perry (2014), "Dogparks and Coffeeshops: Diversity Seeking in Changing Neighborhoods," 46-minute research film, *Association for Consumer Research (ACR) Conference*, Chicago, IL (October).

ENTRY #28

How can looking at the whole picture help you serve customers?

Michael K. Brady

The Carl DeSantis Professor, Florida State University

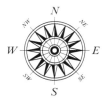

Smart firms know the value of frontline service. After all, "the frontline controls the bottom line," as the saying goes.

The frontline is where customers interact with frontline employees, or FLEs, who then deliver on the firm's brand promise. It is where customers have their first and last impressions of the firm, and it is where problems are resolved and opportunities are uncovered. But, the frontline has changed in ways that make it more complex, exciting, and important than in the past.

For example, as businesses have adopted multi-touchpoint, multi-channel interaction points, the frontline has become multiple frontlines, each with its own set of challenges and opportunities. And technology is involved in frontline exchanges in ways that did not exist a few years ago. Restaurant customers are ordering meals with tablets, artificial intelligence is evolving to include personalized and emotionally appropriate responses to frontline customers, and robots are now sophisticated enough to replace frontline employees. It is expected that this trend will continue to grow, to the point where IBM expects that 85 percent of customer-firm interactions will occur via technology by the year 2020.

Also, customers no longer have singular exchanges with an organization's frontline—instead, they have holistic customer experiences that involve interactions with entities the firm controls (FLEs, lighting, prices) as well as those it does not control (other customers, smart phones). These customer journeys start long before customers engage with frontline staff or click on a firm's website link.

My colleagues and I recently did research that showed customers are very much influenced by experiences they had with other service providers, before they engage with the focal firm. This "emotional spillover" is persistent and it can have dramatic effects on service experiences that occur contiguously, such as air travel where customers go from an Uber ride, to gate agents, to flight attendants, back to Uber, and then to a hotel. A negative experience at any point along the way can ruin the next experience for an unsuspecting service firm and, at the same time, present an opportunity to delight customers who are feeling vulnerable.

So, it is time to rethink the frontline in ways that broaden its scope and includes all of the organization's touchpoints. I am happy to say that this process is underway now. A group of frontline service scholars is working with industry executives to launch an Organizational Frontlines Research (OFR) group. The group includes interested parties with backgrounds in customer service, sales, HR, and technology, to name a few, and the fourth iteration of the OFR conference will occur in 2018.

Early returns from the OFR community include a redefinition of the frontline concept at the intersection of interactions and interfaces. Interactions refer to the events and communications that occur during the firm's contact with a customer whereas interfaces refer to the modes and mediums that define where and how the contact occurs. Firms that will win on the frontline are those that stay ahead of its evolution and learn to manage all aspects of their customer touchpoints.

TAKEAWAYS

- Redefine the frontline in ways that broaden its meaning and includes the many personal and impersonal touchpoints firms have with customers.

- Think about how technology is changing and will continue to change the interactions and interfaces that define your organization's frontline.

- Make sure you understand when customers are willing to trade interpersonal interactions with FLEs for technology-infused contact, and especially when they are not willing to do so.

REFERENCES

Allen, Alexis, Michael Brady, Stacey Robinson, and Clay Voorhees (2015), "One Firm's Loss is Another's Gain: Capitalizing on Other Firms' Service Failures," *Journal of the Academy of Marketing Science*, (September).

The Guardian (2015), "Japan's Robot Hotel," July 15. Available at: www.theguardian.com/world/2015/jul/16/japans-robot-hotel-a-dinosaur-at-reception-a-machine-for-room-service

IBM (2017), "10 Reasons Why AI-Powered, Automated Customer Service Is the Future," April 25. Available at: www.ibm.com/blogs/watson/2017/04/10-reasons-ai-powered-automated-customer-service-future

Lemon, Katherine and Peter Verhoef (2016), "Understanding Customer Experience throughout the Customer Journey," *Journal of Marketing*, (November).

Singh, Jagdip, Michael Brady, Todd Arnold, and Tom Brown (2017), "The Emergent Field of Organizational Frontlines," *Journal of Service Research*, (February).

DESTINATION #5

Customer satisfaction

ENTRY #29

What do customers really want?

Michael Norton

Harold M. Brierley Professor of Business Administration, Harvard Business School

What does it mean to have a "satisfied customer"? In one view, a satisfied customer is one who is loyal: who comes back to buy again and again, whether price increases or not. The character of Walter White on *Breaking Bad* used exactly this logic to measure his success at creating loyal consumers of his product: crystal meth. Over the last decade, a significant shift has occurred both in the academic study of customer satisfaction and in marketing practice. In the form of decreased focus on simply ensuring that customers come back to buy; and increased focus on making customers loyal not solely because they love products but because those products increase another form of satisfaction with their lives. This shift in emphasis is apparent in several domains of consumption, but none have received both the level of academic attention and increased traction in the marketplace more than consuming experiences—from evenings out to dinner, to dream vacations, to trips to space. Millennials in particular demonstrate a decreased focus on stuff—from owning cars to buying houses—and tend to save that money (using services like Uber and Airbnb) in order to save income for experiences. As a result, marketers have increasingly targeted millennials with experience offerings rather than products. As just one example, the enormous success of "sufferfests" —where consumers pay to slog through mud and ice while receiving electric shocks–demonstrates consumers' thirst for experience. Consumers enjoying experiences does not necessarily equate to increased life satisfaction—Walter White's customers enjoyed their meth. But research has documented the many benefits of experiences for consumer well-being. Research by Tom Gilovich, Anat Keinan, and their colleagues has shown that experiences make us happier than stuff:

- Before they occur—waiting for stuff to arrive makes us frustrated, while waiting for experiences to arrive fills us with the positive emotion of anticipation.
- As they occur—stuff tends to be consumed alone, while experiences often serve as a commitment device to spend time with others, a key predictor of well-being.
- After they occur—stuff gets old quickly (there is always a new iPhone lurking on the horizon), but experiences become more and more positive in our memories over time, such that we savor them increasingly over the years.
- And because they make us who we are—experiences help us to fill up our "experiential CVs", allowing us to create an interesting self-narrative.

Experiences offer just one example of an alignment between customer satisfaction and life satisfaction. In my own research with my collaborators, we explore how firms that encourage their customers to give to others through corporate charitable initiative not only create happier customers—because giving to others promotes happiness—but also more loyal customers. The hope is that the trend continues, such that marketers can continue to find products and services that create customers who are happy not only with the firm's offerings, but also with their own lives.

TAKEAWAYS

- Broaden your lens beyond product or service satisfaction, to consider the effect your offering has on consumer well-being and happiness as a whole.

- Do not overlook the strategic opportunity that life-enriching experiences can offer—they may be more sustainable and unique than products.

- Let consumers do good for one another: not only does it make them happy and make the world a better place, it may make them more loyal as well.

REFERENCES

Dunn, Elizabeth and Michael Norton (2013), *Happy Money: The Science of Smarter Spending*. New York: Simon & Schuster.

Dunn, Elizabeth W., Lara B. Aknin, and Michael I. Norton (2008), "Spending Money on Others Promotes Happiness," *Science*, 319, (5870) (March 21), 1687–1688.

Gilovich, Thomas and Amit Kumar (2015), "We'll Always Have Paris: The Hedonic Payoff from Experiential and Material Investments," in Mark Zanna and James Olson (eds.), *Advances in Experimental Social Psychology*, Vol. 51. New York: Elsevier, 147–187.

Keinan, Anat and Ran Kivetz (2011), "Productivity Orientation and the Consumption of Collectable Experiences," *Journal of Consumer Research*, 37 (6), 935–950.

ENTRY #30

How do marketers bring back the voice of the customer?

Kelly D. Martin

Dean's Distinguished Research Fellow and Associate Professor of Marketing, College of Business, Colorado State University

Marketing has witnessed many business solutions that promise to revolutionize how we create and communicate value to our customers. One contemporary trend involves "big data," which has become a proverbial panacea for improving marketing practices. Companies are told that analyzing customer data will revolutionize their business processes and strengthen customer connections. In response, growing numbers of companies are gathering massive amounts of customer data and implementing analytics programs to make sense of this vast information.

Estimates suggest firms dedicate about one-half of all data analytics efforts toward understanding customers. Applications include customer acquisition, building relationships and loyalty enhancements, and product-offering customization, to name just a few. While customers' personal data is focal to providing key insights, to date, there is little conversation about the customer perspective of his or her focal role in companies' big data use. Recently, research has shown that customers may accept provision of their data in exchange for free or better products and services. Customers also understand that companies are using their data to target advertising and other marketing communications uniquely to them. However, customers simultaneously report unprecedented levels of concern about their data privacy and personal information security.

Data privacy research shows that firms' mere access to customer data heightens their feelings of vulnerability, and public opinion polling finds customers are worried their information privacy will erode to the point of non-existence.

Why have customers been neglected from a conversation that is arguably all about them? Marketing research techniques increasingly emphasize patterns and statistical significance, downplaying the value of simple conversations in learning how these practices make customers feel. While such approaches create rigorous understanding of trends and have sharpened future predictions, often missing from this work is the simple voice of the customer, and what he or she wants in this new "big data" environment.

How do marketers bring back the voice of the customer? Interestingly, even small steps can have a big impact. In some of my work on data privacy, by asking customers, we found that out of dozens of constructs they craved the same two dimensions in nearly every application that aroused privacy concerns: they want knowledge of how companies use their information (transparency) and they want some say in that use (control). These two dimensions surfaced again and again, proving superior to dimensions such as fairness, ethics, protection, security, or benevolence in predicting customer outcomes. Perhaps it is no surprise that consumer research on vulnerability identifies transparency and control as the two key components to customer empowerment.

Although we studied transparency and control in data privacy contexts, their benefits have far reaching implications across a variety of marketing domains. We found they had powerful linkages to both cognitive and emotional mechanisms—they enhance trust and reduce feelings of violation. This small attempt at customer goodwill goes a long way by preventing switching, reducing negative word-of-mouth, and promoting loyalty. Yet, transparency and control often require little effort by companies and can be implemented almost immediately.

TAKEAWAYS

- Do not neglect the role of the customer in marketing applications that affect them. This may sound simple, but research shows that customers often are missing from these important decisions.

- View new applications that promise to be a panacea for understanding customers with a skeptical eye. Vast amounts of data do not imply high quality decision outcomes.

- Consider how you can offer your customers greater transparency and control in all the ways you interact with them. Small enhancements on these two dimensions create positive effects.

REFERENCES

Hill, Ronald Paul and Kelly D. Martin (2014), "Broadening the Paradigm of Marketing as Exchange: A Public Policy Perspective," *Journal of Public Policy & Marketing*, 33 (Spring), 17–33.

Martin, Kelly D., Abhishek Borah, and Robert W. Palmatier (2017), "Data Privacy: Effects of Customer and Firm Performance," *Journal of Marketing*, 81 (January), 36–58.

Martin, Kelly D. and Patrick E. Murphy (2017), "The Role of Data Privacy in Marketing," *Journal of the Academy of Marketing Science*, 45 (Spring), 135–155.

ENTRY #31

How does satisficing and justifying among consumers affect marketing?

James W. Gentry
Maurice J. and Alice Hollman College Professor,
University of Nebraska-Lincoln

I was an undergraduate civil engineer who later focused on normative decision theory early in my doctoral education. When I had a great Marketing Research class, I decided to switch to marketing and subsequently became more interested in behavioral decision theory. I believe that decision makers in business should attempt to make decisions correctly, but that most consumers do not do so. Moreover, I am coming to believe that Loewenstein (2001) was correct in asserting that more thought takes place after choice than before it. Thus, the process of justifying decisions post-hoc merits far more emphasis in our approach to consumer decision processes.

An emphasis on choice processes has led some to believe that the marketing system is horrible as we provide too many choice options and create anxiety in consumers. It is hard to argue against there being too many brands in many product categories, but most consumers are not dithering about how to pick the best one. Herb Simon more than 70 years ago made the case that we satisfice rather than maximize. And we know that, *if* we try to analyze offerings systematically, we can use a conjunctive model to narrow the choice set greatly, often without a great deal of effort. Also, we know that more educated middle class consumers do more of the tradeoff analyses (quality versus price) than the lower class, who are more likely to select national brands, as they use brand as a cue for quality. Most of us take short cuts to make choices, often considering how we can justify the choice to ourselves or to others. And in some instances, we avoid making decisions all together; for example, in work (Gentry et al. 1995a, b) on the grief caused by the loss of a loved one, the disorientation felt by the survivors temporarily reduced greatly any planning skills held by them.

Another context questioning generally accepted normative theory is the existence of a debit card; consumer economists are almost unanimous in suggesting that credit cards make more sense due to the leverage offered. However, marketers understood consumers better and the fact that they may have problems with debt if they do not pay off their account each month. Debit cards are now used far more frequently than credit cards. Many college students have learned to leave their credit and debit cards at home when they go out for a night at the bars, so that they will be limited to spending the amount of cash they carry. We play games with ourselves when it comes to spending, and marketers need to understand those games better. A case in point is the seemingly minor differences in banks' perspectives between checking and savings accounts when many consumers consider them to be distinct, with savings generally seen as being somewhat sacred. Poyner and Hawes (2009) in their piece on motivated categorization note how the same object can be classified as a necessity or a luxury, with the former being far easier to justify.

Thus, I have come to believe that we need to drop the illusion that consumers try to maximize anything, and consider in more depth why consumers really make the choices they do. Parker, Lehmann, and Xie (2016) offer us the decision comfort approach, which I see as having much potential. Marketers can make consumers more comfortable, in part at least, by emphasizing aspects of the product or service that make choice more easily justifiable. Marketers should think about that so that consumers will not have to.

TAKEAWAYS

- Humans try to avoid thinking.
- We make good enough decisions for the most part.
- We need to justify those decisions to ourselves and to others.

REFERENCES

Gentry, James W., Patricia F. Kennedy, Catherine Paul, and Ronald Paul Hill (1995a). "Family Transitions During Grief: Discontinuities in Household Consumption Patterns," *Journal of Business Research*, 34 (September), 67–79.

Gentry, James W., Patricia F. Kennedy, Catherine Paul, and Ronald Paul Hill (1995b), "The Vulnerability of Those in Grief: Implications for Public Policy," *Journal of Public Policy and Marketing*, 14 (Spring), 128–142.

Loewenstein, George (2001), "The Creative Destruction of Decision Research," *Journal of Consumer Research*, 24 (December), 499–505.

Parker, Jeffrey, Donald Lehmann, and Y. Xie (2016), "Decision Comfort," *Journal of Consumer Research*, 41 (June), 113–133.

Poynor, Cait and Kelly L. Hawes (2009), "Lines in the Sand: The Role of Motivated Categorization in the Pursuit of Self-Control Goals," *Journal of Consumer Research*, 35 (February), 772–787.

ENTRY #32

How can you better predict future consumer preferences when consumers often have trouble doing so?

Rebecca Hamilton

Michael G. and Robin Psaros Chair in Business Administration and Professor of Marketing, McDonough School of Business, Georgetown University

Marketing researchers often ask consumers to predict what they will want at a later time. For example, before introducing a new product, they seek input on which features to include, where to sell the product and how much to charge. A fundamental assumption of this approach is that consumers will be able to accurately predict their preferences at some time in the future for a product that may not yet exist.

Yet, evidence suggests that consumers can make large and systematic errors when predicting their preferences. Before they use a product, consumers are attracted to models that have a large number of features, but after they have used the product, they tend to prefer products with fewer features that are easier to use. When considering a leisure activity such as going to a museum, consumers often predict that they will enjoy the experience less if they go alone rather than with another person. Yet, consumers report enjoying such an activity just as much when they go alone as when they go with someone else. When choosing a replacement for a choice that becomes unavailable, consumers tend to choose substitutes highly similar to their initial choice, even though consuming a more dissimilar substitute more effectively reduces their desire for their initial choice.

Why do consumers have trouble predicting their future preferences? One reason is that consumers think differently about products and activities before and after they use or experience them. Before they use a product, they think about it abstractly; they tend to prefer a lot of features that can do many things. After they have used a product, they think more concretely; they value ease of use much more. This change in preferences is consistent with research on psychological distance, which suggests that when psychological distance is high (considering other people, events in the future, distant locations, and imagined experiences), consumers think more abstractly and focus on desirability, but when psychological distance is low (considering oneself, right now, the current location, and an actual experience), consumers think more concretely and focus on feasibility.

If consumers themselves make incorrect predictions about their future preferences, how can we, as marketing researchers, predict their preferences? It is critical for researchers to consider whether consumers will be able to provide accurate responses to the questions they ask. Consider a research team who surveyed college students, asking whether they were influenced by ads on Facebook. None of the respondents said they were influenced by Facebook ads, so they concluded that Facebook ads do not work despite Facebook attracting billions of dollars in ad revenue. These researchers chose the wrong method: consumers may not know or want to admit they are influenced by ads. Using a direct method, such as a survey, interview or focus group, is not a good choice. A better approach is to use an indirect method, like an experiment, which compares purchases of consumers exposed to (vs. not exposed to) an ad on Facebook. An experiment does not require consumers to predict their behavior, allowing researchers to determine whether consumer behavior is being influenced even if consumers do not know (or will not admit) that it is.

When consumers have trouble predicting their preferences, it is critical to ask questions indirectly, such as by using experiments. Experiments allow us to learn that consumers prefer simple products once they have had a chance to use them, that they enjoy themselves when they go to an art gallery alone, and that they want an initially desired product less after consuming a dissimilar than a similar substitute. Asking consumers directly simply gives researchers the wrong answer.

TAKEAWAYS

- For marketers and researchers, choosing the right method to answer a research question is critical. Think carefully about how accurately consumers can respond to the questions you are asking.

- As consumers, it is hard for us to imagine how we will feel in a different environment. This makes it hard for us to predict their preferences at a different time, in a different place, or in a different social context. When making an important decision, do your best to put yourself in the position of using the product or engaging in an activity, and you will be more likely to make a good choice.

REFERENCES

Arens, Zachary G. and Rebecca W. Hamilton (2016), "Why Focusing on the Similarity of Substitutes Leaves a Lot to Be Desired," *Journal of Consumer Research*, 43 (October), 448–459.

Hamilton, Rebecca W. (2015), "Bridging Psychological Distance," *Harvard Business Review*, 93 (March), 116–119.

Hamilton, Rebecca W., Roland T. Rust, and Chekitan S. Dev (2017), "Which Features Retain Customers?" *MIT Sloan Management Review*, 58 (Winter), 79–84.

Hamilton, Rebecca W. and Debora V. Thompson (2007), "Is There a Substitute for Direct Experience? Comparing Consumers' Preferences After Direct and Indirect Product Experiences," *Journal of Consumer Research*, 34 (December), 546–555.

Ratner, Rebecca K. and Rebecca W. Hamilton (2015), "Inhibited From Bowling Alone," *Journal of Consumer Research*, 42 (August), 266–283.

Rust, Roland T., Debora V. Thompson, and Rebecca W. Hamilton (2006), "Defeating Feature Fatigue," *Harvard Business Review*, 84 (February), 98–107.

Thompson, Debora V., Rebecca W. Hamilton, and Roland T. Rust (2005), "Feature Fatigue: When Product Capabilities Become Too Much of a Good Thing," *Journal of Marketing Research*, 42 (November), 431–442.

ENTRY #33

How do your prices actually affect consumers?

Ryan Hamilton

Associate Professor of Marketing, Goizueta Business School, Emory University

Several years ago, Whole Foods bought a store location in an up-and-coming Boston neighborhood from a regional grocery store chain called Hi Lo Foods. Then came the protests. Flyers were distributed, neighborhood meetings descended into yelling and chanting, and an honest to goodness, sign-wielding picket line formed in front of the renovation site. Chief among the protesters' concerns was the fact that the prices at Whole Foods were so much higher than those of the store it was replacing. How were the residents going to feed their families when faced with such astronomical prices?

Except . . . when an intrepid reporter from the Boston Globe actually went out and compared prices at grocery stores across the city, he found that prices at Whole Foods were less than 5% higher than at the Hi Lo it would be replacing. (By way of comparison, Hi Lo was about 12% higher than the Stop & Shop in the same neighborhood.) Now, a 5% price increase is nothing to sniff at. But it also rarely elicits angry street protests.

Those angry Bostonians were likely not protesting Whole Foods's actual prices, but instead Whole Foods's reputation for high prices. In point of fact, Whole Foods's prices are relatively competitive: a recent study conducted by Wells Fargo comparing a basket of 100 items found that Whole Foods's prices beat Safeway by 7%, Sprouts Farmers Market by 3%, The Fresh Market by 14%, and Amazon Fresh by 27%. Whole Foods's prices were only 4% higher than Trader Joe's. But also in point of fact, none of those rigorous price comparisons matter to most consumers, because in their hearts they know that "Whole Paycheck" charges unconscionably high prices.

A firm's reputation for pricing is known formally as its price image, defined as the impression that consumers form about the overall price level of a retailer or manufacturer. And research dating back at least as far as the 1960s has found that consumers are surprisingly inaccurate in their price image impressions.

These inaccuracies are caused by two different sources of bias. The first source of bias is the way that people process price information. Research suggests that not all prices are equally important when forming a price image, and in particular, the prices that receive more attention, such as those of purchased items, will be more influential. But it is worse than just a biased selection of prices: customers' evaluations of prices are not objective, but can be influenced by the context, including the prices of surrounding items. For example, the presence of a high priced, super premium toaster on the shelf, could drive down the evaluation of the price of the utilitarian toaster a shopper actually buys—and thereby lower the price image of the retailer.

The second source of bias that can cause consumers to form inaccurate price image impressions is the non-price information they incorporate into their impressions. From the moment customers walk into a store for the first time, they are bombarded with information that they can use to anticipate the store's prices: the upscale décor, the modern lighting, the travertine floors, the friendly helpful sales people, the location in an upscale mall . . . It is entirely possible for customers to form a price image of a store before they even see their first price tag.

Given the way these impressions are formed, marketers should not be surprised when consumers' price images are off. They should anticipate these sources of bias and manage around them.

TAKEAWAYS

- Do not assume that customers' price image impressions of a brand or retailer are accurate reflections of actual price levels. Price images can be biased by all kinds of things.

- Managing price image requires more than just managing prices. Managing price image requires managing all the price-related associations customers have in memory. In this way, managing price image is more like managing a brand than it is managing prices.

- Price images tend to be self-reinforcing. Once customers think your prices are high, even objectively low prices may not be enough to persuade them.

REFERENCES

Brown, F. E. (1969), "Price Image versus Price Reality," *Journal of Marketing Research*, 6 (May), 185–191.

Hamilton, Ryan and Alexander Chernev (2013), "Low Prices are Just the Beginning: Price Image in Retail Management," *Journal of Marketing*, 70 (November), 1–20.

Hamilton, Ryan and Alexander Chernev (2010), "The Impact of Product Line Extensions and Consumer Goals on the Formation of Price Image," *Journal of Marketing Research*, 47 (February), 51–62.

ENTRY #34

How do you create the ultimate customer experience?

Kay Lemon

Accenture Professor, Boston College

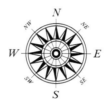

There has been much focus on customer experience and the customer journey—not just the path to purchase, but through post-purchase, usage and beyond. Customer experience has become so complex, and yet so observable, through innumerable channels, touchpoints and data types. The amount of "input" we now have on the customer journey is overwhelming.

How can we make sense of the complexity? And do we even need to? Should we focus significant attention and resources on customer experience and the customer journey? Or is it perhaps just a fad?

Here is the key: as researchers and marketers, we have been focusing on and learning about the customer experience and customer journey for decades! What is needed is to integrate all we have learned about how customers build relationships with firms, and to view these insights through a customer experience lens.

In our research, we have developed a framework to (hopefully) begin to make sense of the complexity. First, it is necessary to identify the broad-brush stages of the customer journey: we focus on (1) pre-purchase, (2) purchase, and (3) post-purchase. Clearly, this is a significant oversimplification—but that is the point. Get the big picture first; then focus on the (important) small details.

Second, recognize that not all touchpoints are the same across the customer's journey—and that the firm's ability to control these touchpoints differs. We have identified four distinct types of touchpoints:

1. Brand-owned: consider the traditional 4Ps (product, promotion, price, place)—the firm has most control of this type.
2. Partner-owned: media partners, technology partners, partners in the service network—the firm has some control and input.
3. Customer-owned: customer motivations, past experiences, emotions—the firm has very little control or input.
4. Social/Independent/External: environmental factors, macro-factors, social connections, even social media—the firm has some input but no control.

Equipped with this relatively simple framing (stages and touchpoints) the firm can now begin to design, manage and measure the customer experience. Importantly, do not throw away what you already know, or what you are already doing. Rather, integrate it into the stages and touchpoints framework.

How? A few examples can illustrate. Attribution models help identify critical touchpoints in the pre-purchase and purchase stages—especially for brand-owned touchpoints. User experience (UX) studies inform the post-purchase stage of the journey—especially regarding customer-owned and social/independent/external touchpoints. Operational measures and web metrics are also quite useful to layer on. And you probably already measure satisfaction or NPS. Keep it up. Just recognize what specific aspect of the experience or journey you are measuring and integrate it. Then . . . see what you are missing and what you do not yet understand—these represent the real learning opportunities.

A few things we (as a field) have learned may help you on your journey. First, understand the customer journey from the customer's point of view—this is actually quite harder than it appears. Second, take the customer's context and broader network (in which the experience occurs) into account. Third, linkage models—that identify how the firm's actions influence customer perceptions, emotions and behaviors—which then, in turn, influence firm outcomes—are quite useful. Fourth, recognize that multiple measures are typically better than single measures.

Finally, remember that you probably know a lot more about the customer experience throughout the customer journey than you think. And relatively simple, usable frameworks can help to make the complex (and messy) more manageable.

Creating the ultimate customer experience **113**

TAKEAWAYS

- When designing a customer experience and customer journey, do not forget to imagine it (all the way through) from the customer's perspective.

- Remember that each customer experiences her or his own journey; recognize the context in which each customer's experience occurs and tailor the experience to that context.

- Be careful to understand what aspect of the customer experience you are capturing with any measure—and, when possible, use multiple measures.

REFERENCES

Bolton, Ruth N., Katherine N. Lemon, and Peter C. Verhoef (2004), "The Theoretical Underpinnings of Customer Asset Management: A Framework and Propositions for Future Research," *Journal of the Academy of Marketing Science*, 32 (Summer), 271–293.

De Keyser, Arne, Katherine N. Lemon, Timothy L. Keiningham, and Phil Klaus (2015), "A Framework for Understanding and Managing the Customer Experience," *Marketing Science Institute Reports Working Paper Series*, 15-121.

De Haan, Evert, Peter C. Verhoef, and Thorsten Wiesel (2015), "The Predictive Ability of Different Customer Feedback Metrics for Retention," *International Journal of Research in Marketing*, 32 (2), 195–206.

Lemon, Katherine N. and Peter C. Verhoef (2016), "Understanding Customer Experience Throughout the Customer Journey," *Journal of Marketing*, 80 (November), 69–96.

Rust, Roland T., Katherine N. Lemon, and Valarie A. Zeithaml (2004), "Return on Marketing: Using Customer Equity to Focus Marketing Strategy," *Journal of Marketing*, 68 (January), 109–127.

ENTRY #35

How do you measure service quality?

Valarie A. Zeithaml
The David S. Van Pelt Family Distinguished Professor,
University of North Carolina at Chapel Hill

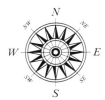

Although researchers and companies in the era of quality were eager to find ways to measure service quality, insufficient research had been conducted to begin measurement. When Parsu Parasuraman, Len Berry and I began our work on service quality, very little literature existed. Early writing on the topic of consumer perceptions suggested that service quality results from a comparison of what customers feel a service provider should offer (i.e., their expectations) with how the provider actually performs. This notion that service quality is a function of the expectations-performance gap was reinforced by our qualitative, multi-sector study involving twelve customer focus group interviews—three in each of four different service sectors (retail banking, credit card, stock brokerage, and appliance repair and maintenance)—that explored how customers assessed service quality. Based on common insights from the focus groups, we formally defined service quality as perceived by customers as the degree and direction of discrepancy between customers' service perceptions and expectations. Ten dimensions were repeatedly mentioned by customers across the focus groups.

As is the case with any qualitative research, we recognized that what we found in our first study should be examined empirically. We followed the exploratory study with empirical analysis, which produced SERVQUAL, a twenty-two item, five-factor service quality instrument. In the empirical analysis, three of the original ten dimensions remained intact in the final set of five dimensions. These three dimensions were tangibles, reliability, and responsiveness. The remaining seven original dimensions were clustered into two broader dimensions. Based on the content of the items under these two broader dimensions, we labeled them assurance and empathy.

Hundreds of published studies have used SERVQUAL and adaptations of it in a variety of contexts. Numerous descendants of SERVQUAL in various industries have been developed including DINESERVE in the restaurant industry, LODGSERV in the hospitality industry, and LibQUAL in the library field. In addition, consultants have used the instrument, which they termed RATER (the acronym represents the five factors of service quality). Subsequent papers on SERVQUAL clarified aspects that were contested, leading us to continue to publish improved scales.

In the first phase of our research, we also developed our approach to viewing the delivery of service quality in a structured and integrated way: the gaps model of service quality. The gaps model positions the key concepts, strategies, and decisions in delivering quality service in a manner that begins with the customer and builds the organization's tasks around what is needed to close the gap between customer expectations and perceptions.

When we created the model, I did not realize how useful it would be in my research, teaching, and practice. As a comprehensive framework for viewing all strategies and tactics necessary for understanding and delivering quality service, it has been an endless source of ideas for research. Virtually all services marketing strategies fall somewhere in the four provider gaps, as do service operations and human resource strategies.

TAKEAWAYS

- Perceived service quality can be measured and tracked.

- The gaps model of service quality provides a comprehensive strategy framework for improving service.

- Many versions of SERVQUAL for different industries exist and would be a good foundation for measuring service.

REFERENCES

Parasuraman, A., Leonard L. Berry, and Valerie A. Zeithaml (1993), "More on Improving Service Quality Measurement," *Journal of Retailing*, 69 (1), 140–147.

Parasuraman, A., Valerie A. Zeithaml, and Leonard L. Berry (1994), "Alternative Scales for Measuring Service Quality: A Comparative Assessment Based on Psychometric and Diagnostic Criteria," *Journal of Retailing*, 70 (3), 201–230.

Parasuraman, A., Valerie A. Zeithaml, and Leonard L. Berry (1994), "Reassessment of Expectations as a Comparison Standard in Measuring Service Quality: Implications of Future Research," *Journal of Marketing*, 58 (1), 111–124.

Parasuraman, A., Valerie A. Zeithaml, and Leonard L. Berry (1988), "SERVQUAL: A Multiple-Item Scale for Measuring Service Quality," *Journal of Retailing*, 64 (1), 12–40.

Parasuraman, A., Valerie A. Zeithaml, and Leonard L. Berry (1985), "A Conceptual Model of Service Quality and Its Implications for Future Research," *Journal of Marketing*, 49, 41–50.

Parasuraman, A., Valerie A. Zeithaml, and Arvind Malhotra (2005), "e-SERVQUAL: A Multiple-Item Scale for Assessing Electronic Service Quality," *Journal of Service Research*, 7 (3), 213–233.

Zeithaml, Valerie A. (1988), "Consumer Perceptions of Price, Quality, and Value: A Means-end Model and Synthesis of the Evidence," *Journal of Marketing*, 52 (2), 2–22.

Zeithaml, Valerie A., Leonard L. Berry, and Parasuraman, A. (1996), "The Behavioral Consequences of Service Quality," *Journal of Marketing*, 60 (2), 31–46.

Zeithaml, Valerie A., Mary Jo Bitner, and Dwayne Gremler (2018), *Services Marketing: Integrating Customer Focus Across the Firm, seventh edition*, New York: Irwin/Mc-Graw Hill.

Zeithaml, Valerie A., A. Parasuraman, and Leonard L. Berry (1990), *Delivering Quality Service: Balancing Customer Expectations and Perceptions*, New York: Free Press.

DESTINATION #6

Consumer wellbeing

ENTRY #36

How can marketing spark change in consumer health?

Cornelia (Connie) Pechmann

Professor of Marketing, The Paul Merage School of Business, University of California Irvine

Marketers should not take ourselves too seriously because we do not save lives, right? I was told that as a doctoral student, but still I wanted to save lives. So, I decided to study marketing that relates to tobacco consumption. Also ignoring the advice that marketing academics cannot get large grants, I obtained several seed grants from California, then a federal seed grant, and finally a large multi-million dollar grant from the US National Institutes of Health for my tobacco research.

My first project was to study whether cigarette ads played any role in encouraging adolescents to start smoking, because pre-eminent marketing scholars were testifying in courts that cigarette ads played no role in smoking initiation. My studies showed that non-smoking adolescents were affected by cigarette ads, but only indirectly because the ads altered their perceptions of peers who smoked. The attractive models in cigarette ads made peers who smoked look cool, and so youth wanted to smoke to look cool too. Psychologists call this a priming effect, but it was a novel example of it, because adolescents do not admit to having the positive smoker stereotypes that are primed or made salient by cigarette ads.

My next project determined that seeing young adult actors smoking in movies doubled adolescents' intent to smoke. However, showing an antismoking ad before a movie that portrayed smokers as uncool caused "reverse priming" and inoculated adolescents from the attractive smoker models. Actor Arnold Schwarzenegger was California's governor at the time, and so his officials reached out to movie studios and persuaded them to include antismoking ads before movies with smoking for adolescents, on the movie DVDs.

I have also studied different antismoking and anti-marijuana ads to figure out which ones work best. The ads that consistently did the best portrayed smokers and drug users in a negative light, or alternatively portrayed non-smokers and non-drug users positively. Moreover, using both positive and negative appeals reached different segments of adolescents. These results helped guide several ad campaigns, though I encountered resistance from the national antismoking campaign, Truth, because its officials decided from the onset to use anti-industry ads, not based on research, but based on their experiences during the anti-establishment anti-Vietnam war era.

With my large federal grant, I am working on Tweet2Quit, which is a program I devised that sets up social media-based quit-smoking groups. We put 20 smokers that want to quit in a private Twitter group, we tell them to quit within a week and to support each other for three months, and we send them daily automated messages to encourage continued engagement, which has been our greatest challenge. Our seed research found Tweet2Quit doubled quit-smoking rates, but we are perfecting the program and expanding to women-only groups. It is gratifying to hear so many participants say Tweet2Quit has been invaluable to their quit efforts. If it works well, the US government's smoke-free.gov website hopes to offer Tweet2Quit for free. How is that for saving lives?

TAKEAWAYS

- Marketing academics can obtain large government grants for research that directly improves health.

- Ads can work indirectly, by altering or priming social perceptions, which then affect consumption.

- Movies can have a profound impact on adolescents, especially in influencing lifestyle decisions.

- Adolescents are affected by ads showing positive or negative characterizations of peer product users.

- Social media-based group programs can promote healthier lifestyles but engagement is a challenge.

REFERENCES

Lakon, Cynthia M., Cornelia Pechmann, Cheng Wang, Li Pan, Kevin Delucchi, and Judith J. Prochaska (2016), "Mapping Engagement in Twitter-Based Support Networks for Adult Smoking Cessation," *American Journal of Public Health*, 106 (8), 1374–1380.

Pechmann, Cornelia and Chuan-Fong Shih (1999), "Smoking Scenes in Movies and Antismoking Advertisements before Movies: Effects on Youth," *Journal of Marketing*, 63 (3), 1–13.

Pechmann, Cornelia., Kevin Delucchi, Cynthia M. Lakon, and Judith J. Prochaska (2017), "Randomised Controlled Trial Evaluation of Tweet2Quit: A Social Network Quit-smoking Intervention," *Tobacco Control*, 26, 188–194.

Pechmann, Cornelia and Susan J. Knight (2002), "An Experimental Investigation of the Joint Effects of Advertising and Peers on Adolescents' Beliefs and Intentions About Cigarette Consumption," *Journal of Consumer Research*, 29 (1), 5–19.

Pechmann, Cornelia, Li Pan, Kevin Delucchi, Cynthia M. Lakon, and Judith J. Prochaska (2015), "Development of a Twitter-Based Intervention for Smoking Cessation That Encourages High-Quality Social Media Interactions Via Automessages," *Journal of Medical Internet Research*, 17 (2), e50, 1–11.

Pechmann, Cornelia, Guangzhi Zhao, Marvin E. Goldberg, and Ellen Thomas Reibling (2003), "What to Convey in Antismoking Advertisements for Adolescents? The Use of Protection Motivation Theory to Identify Effective Message Themes," *Journal of Marketing*, 67 (2), 1–18.

Pezzuti, Todd, Dante Pirouz, and Cornelia Pechmann (2015), "The Effects of Advertising Models for Age-Restricted Products and Self-Concept Discrepancy on Advertising Outcomes among Young Adolescents," *Journal of Consumer Psychology*, 25 (3), 519–529.

Zhao, Guangzhi and Cornelia Pechmann (2007), "The Impact of Regulatory Focus on Adolescents' Response to Antismoking Advertising Campaigns," *Journal of Marketing Research*, 44 (4), 671–687.

ENTRY #37

What is the best strategy to employ when conducting healthy food marketing?

Pierre Chandon

L'Oréal Chaired Professor of Marketing, Innovation and Creativity, INSEAD

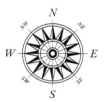

Traditional policy solutions to the obesity epidemic (warnings, labels, taxes, bans), despite their usefulness, generate strong resistance because they are perceived as restricting choice and stifling business. Traditional industry response, food reformulation, is mistrusted on both hedonic or health grounds and can lead to overeating because of "health halos."

More fundamentally, obesity is largely driven by ever-increasing food portion sizes. Yet, our efforts to fight it have focused on trying to influence what people eat instead of how much they eat. It is time to consider two other approaches, focused on fighting obesity by making people happier to spend more for less food, a triple win for public health, business, and eating enjoyment. Less size: improve the perception of reasonable portion and package sizes. Food portions and packages have increased enormously. Part of the reason why we accept this is that supersized portions appear smaller than they are because our brains are very bad at geometry. Yet, because our brains tend to add (rather than multiply) the changes in dimension, we perceive that object to be only 50% to 70% bigger. The net results are huge portions that consumers don't see and are not willing to pay for, overeating, and food waste, a total lose–lose scenario. Unfortunately, our brains are more accurate when it comes to downsizing because they now have two reference points: the original size and the knowledge that sizes are always bigger than zero. To encourage people to prefer—and pay for—smaller portions, one strategy is to add small sizes to the range available, making the old "small" a "medium". Another approach is to brand sizes in a way that communicates volume, like Starbucks branding its smallest size, the "tall" cup. Finally, my research has shown that elongating rather than shortening food packaging and portions masks size reduction and greatly facilitates downsizing.

More pleasure: focus on the sensory enjoyment of eating rather than on satiation or value for money. The second approach focuses on making people choose and actually prefer to pay more for smaller portions. Most people choose large portions because they are good value and will not leave them hungry. However, they forget that sensory pleasure peaks after the few first bites, and that it is the last bite that determines the overall enjoyment of the food. Hence, people often eat portions that are too large from a pleasure standpoint. Ask people to remember the sensory experience that they had when eating hedonic food has led school kids, French and American adults, and restaurant customers to choose the smaller portions of desserts that were actually the best size for eating enjoyment. Fat and calories information also made people choose smaller desserts but feel bad about it, reducing their willingness to pay for the experience. In contrast, more vivid menu descriptions made people choose smaller portions and feel good about it, making them willing to pay more for less food. That is a triple win for health, business, and eating pleasure.

TAKEAWAYS

- Pleasure can be the ally, not the enemy, of healthier (more reasonable) eating.

- People have strong preference for what to eat, but not for how much to eat (they just want a "normal" size).

- Our brain is bad at estimating quantity. Perceived size grows more slowly than actual size.

- People spot quantity decreases a lot more accurately than quantity increases.

- Overall eating enjoyment of food is not the sum, but the average, of the pleasure derived from each bite.

REFERENCES

Chandon, Pierre and Nailya Ordabayeva (2017), "The Accuracy of Less: Natural Bounds Explain Why Quantity Decreases Are Estimated More Accurately than Quantity Increases," *Journal of Experimental Psychology: General*, 146 (2), 250–268.

Chandon, Pierre and Nailya Ordabayeva (2009), "Supersize in One Dimension, Downsize in Three Dimensions: Effects of Spatial Dimensionality on Size Perceptions and Preferences," *Journal of Marketing Research*, 46 (6), 739–753.

Chandon, Pierre and Brian Wansink (2012) "Does Food Marketing Need to Make Us Fat? A Review and Solutions," *Nutrition Reviews*, 70 (10), 571–593.

Chandon, Pierre and Brian Wansink (2007), "The Biasing Health Halos of Fast Food Restaurant Health Claims: Lower Calorie Estimates and Higher Side-Dish Consumption Intentions," *Journal of Consumer Research*, 34 (October), 301–314.

Cornil, Yann and Pierre Chandon (2016), "Pleasure as an Ally of Healthy Eating? Contrasting Visceral and Epicurean Eating Pleasure and Their Association with Portion Size Preferences and Wellbeing," *Appetite*, 104, 52–59.

Cornil, Yann and Pierre Chandon (2016), "Pleasure as a Substitute for Size: How Multisensory Imagery Can Make People Happier with Smaller Food Portions," *Journal of Marketing Research*, 53 (5), 847–864.

Ordabayeva, Nailya and Pierre Chandon (2016), "In the Eye of the Beholder: Visual Biases in Package and Portion Size Perceptions," *Appetite*, 103, 450–457.

ENTRY #38

How does price influence food decision making?

Kelly L. Haws
Associate Professor of Marketing and Chancellor's Faculty Fellow, Owen Graduate School of Management, Vanderbilt University

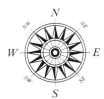

Consumers make dozens of food decisions each and every day, involving trade-offs between taste, healthiness, convenience, price, serving sizes, variety, cultural norms, social acceptance, and many other factors. In order to make this process survivable, consumers apply a wide range decision shortcuts and intuitions. As researchers, we tend to simplify decision making in order to understand how one or two factors at a time impact what consumers buy and eat. Ultimately, the calculus is more complicated and the consequences often severe, as evidenced by unhealthy outcomes including obesity, chronic disease, and overall reduced well-being. So, what do we know and what might we often overlook that can contribute to understanding food decision making patterns?

Two factors in food decisions that often receive top billing are taste and health, and the underlying self-control conflicts that emerge. Prior research has shown that consumers tend to hold the belief that unhealthy foods are tastier than healthy ones, and such intuitions can have a powerful effect on our decisions. However, some of our recent research has focused on what is arguably a more marketing specific and pragmatic criterion in food decision making: price. Researchers have identified geographical areas in the U.S. in which access to fresh produce is limited while fast food options are abundant (often called food deserts). Yet, the role of pricing in making food decisions is a much larger and not always well understood. Herein, I briefly consider three examples based upon my research with various colleagues.

First, consumers have frequently been exposed to "supersized" pricing in which larger sizes of food products and beverages are accompanied by prices that are cheaper per unit. We find that consumers often justify the purchase of these larger sizes through the greater perceptions of value for their dollar. Unfortunately, much research has shown that merely having larger quantities available leads to increased consumption. And most supersized pricing seems to apply to less healthy alternatives.

The second example builds on different portion sizes and the related pricing schemes. Specifically, the increasing presence of calorie labels (as mandated by recent legislation in many cases) on restaurant menus has spurred research about the effects of this health information. We add to this understanding by layering in portion size options and pricing. When pricing is linear (that is, a "half-sized" portion costs half as much as a full-sized one), then calorie information had the intended effect of reducing calories ordered. However, when the pricing instead reflected a supersized pricing scheme, calorie information no longer influenced ordering, rather pricing dominated.

Third, one of the intuitions that consumers often utilize in making decisions in ambiguous food environments is that healthier products are more expensive. While this may hold up as truth in specific contexts (e.g., organic foods), this intuition is frequently over applied and possibly leads people to give up on trying to eat healthy foods when doing so is viewed as a threat to their budgets. The bottom line here is that consumers use prices to help infer healthiness, again suggesting a central role of pricing in food decision making.

Overall, understanding how consumers navigate the complexities of food decision making day in and day out is critical to understanding long-term patterns of consumption. Studying all inputs together is quite challenging, but I would argue that we cannot lose sight of the financial impact on consumers.

TAKEAWAYS

- Food decision making is complicated, and therefore understanding the rules of thumb that guide consumers is crucial to understanding patterns of behavior.

- Trade-offs are a real or perceived part of food decision making for consumers, and consumers often perceive conflicts between health, taste, and price.

- Although the relationship between price and other food-related characteristics is complex, we must remember to consider the financial impact or burden on consumers.

REFERENCES

Haws, Kelly L., Rebecca Walker Reczek, and Kevin L. Sample (2017), "Healthy Diets Make Empty Wallets: The Healthy = Expensive Intuition," *Journal of Consumer Research*, 43 (6), 992–1007.

Haws, Kelly L. and Peggy J. Liu (2016), "Half-size Me? How Calorie and Price Information Influence on Restaurant Menus with Both Half and Full Entrée Portion Sizes," *Appetite* (103), 441–449.

Haws, Kelly L. and Karen Page Winterich (2013), "When Value Trumps Health in a Supersized World," *Journal of Marketing*, 77 (3), 48–64.

ENTRY #39

What factors influence over-consumption and how can marketers use this information to improve customers' wellbeing?

Maura L. Scott

Madeline Duncan Rolland Associate Professor of Business Administration, Florida State University

Every day, individuals encounter numerous factors that influence their over-consumption of products and services, and this can affect their health and well-being. The focus on consumer well-being is part of an emerging area in marketing called Transformative Consumer Research. I examine these phenomena using field and laboratory experiments to provide new theoretical insights relevant to other scholars, policy makers, consumers, and companies. I study consumers' psychological states (e.g., body-esteem) and environmental factors (e.g., product and package design), and their consequences on downstream behaviors (calorie intake, compensatory consumption).

A consumer's psychological relationship with food can influence responses to food packaging. In one paper, we found that dietary restraint (e.g., chronic dieting) influenced how much people ate from mini-packs. Restrained eaters consumed more calories when eating smaller morsels from smaller packages, than when eating larger morsels from larger packages. This suggests that some package designs that are positioned as diet foods can backfire on restrained eaters. In another paper, we studied the effects of cute designs on indulgent consumption. In one study, we found that consumers ate more ice-cream when they scooped it with a cute (vs. neutral) ice-cream scoop, because whimsically cute products make people think of fun and indulgence. Building on these findings, another paper has examined how to improve how people approach food. We proposed a shift from an emphasis on restraint and restrictions to a more positive, holistic understanding of the role of food in consumers lives.

My research also examines how goal setting can help consumers stick to health goals such as losing weight. In one study with members of a weight loss program, we found that the goal type can influence motivation over time. High-low range goals (e.g., lose 2–4 pounds) resulted in greater motivation than single number goals (e.g., lose 3 pounds). Literacy is another factor influencing health goals. We found that patients with lower medical literacy levels showed significantly greater willingness to comply with their physician's recommendations when the patient was actively involved in their care.

Closely related to the question of health and well-being is the issue of body-esteem. My research on clothing sizes uncovered how female shoppers cope with body-esteem threats that come from undesired clothing sizes. Because clothing sizes are not standardized, when a woman visits a new store and expects to wear a certain size, there is a chance that the expected size may be too small or too large. Loose clothing can be flattering, and she may be willing to pay more for the clothing. However, when the clothing is too small, this can create a body-esteem threat. We found that consumers felt threatened when the clothing was too tight, but they sought to restore their body-esteem by seeking non-sized appearance enhancing items such as jewelry. Interestingly, these consumers did not seek products that enhance other types of self-esteem, such as intelligence-esteem.

TAKEAWAYS

- Consumers have an ongoing journey to achieve an improved well-being as they incorporate products and services in their lives.

- Consumers can set high-low range goals that provide both a challenge and a sense of attainability, and this can help consumers stick with their goals over time.

- Engaging consumers in their health goals, especially lower literacy consumers, can result in a positive eustress experience, which helps to improve compliance with expert advice.

- Marketers have the opportunity to develop offerings that enhance well-being and quality of life, while also performing on key metrics such as customer satisfaction, customer loyalty, brand attitudes, and profitability.

REFERENCES

Block, Lauren, Sonya Grier, Terry Childers, Brennan Davis, Jane Ebert, Shiriki Kumanyika, Russ Laczniak, Jane Machin, Carol Motley, Laura Peracchio, Simone Pettigrew, Maura L. Scott, and Mirjam van Ginkel Bieshaar (2011), "From Nutrients to Nurturance: A Conceptual Introduction to Food Well-Being," *Journal of Public Policy & Marketing*, 30 (1), 5–13.

Hoegg, JoAndrea, Maura L. Scott, Andrea C. Morales, and Darren W. Dahl, (2014), "The Flip Side of Vanity Sizing: How Consumers Respond to and Compensate for Larger than Expected Clothing Sizes," *Journal of Consumer Psychology*, 24 (1), 70–78.

Mende, Martin, Maura L. Scott, Mary Jo Bitner, and Amy L. Ostrom, (2017), "Activating Customers for Better Coproduction Outcomes: The Interplay of Firm-Assigned Workload, Service Literacy, Eustress, and Organizational Support," *Journal of Public Policy & Marketing*, 36 (1), 137–155.

Nenkov, Gergana Y. and Maura L. Scott, (2014) "So Cute I Could Eat It Up: Priming Effects of Cute Products on Indulgent Consumption," *Journal of Consumer Research*, 41 (2), 326–341.

Scott, Maura L. and Stephen M. Nowlis, (2013), "The Effect of Goal Specificity on Consumer Goal Reengagement," *Journal of Consumer Research*, 40 (3), 444–459.

Scott, Maura L., Stephen M. Nowlis, Naomi Mandel, and Andrea C. Morales (2008), "The Effect of Reduced Food Sizes and Packages on the Consumption Behavior of Restrained Eaters and Unrestrained Eaters," *Journal of Consumer Research*, 35 (3), 391–405.

ENTRY #40

How do female mannequins impact consumers?

Jennifer J. Argo

Carthy Professor of Marketing, University of Alberta

A common belief in the apparel industry is that mannequins are beneficial communication tools. Indeed, mannequins are described as one of the most powerful marketing tools available to fashion retailers and there are only a handful of clothing stores into which a consumer might enter that a mannequin is not present. Given the prominent role they play in an industry that is valued at more than $3 trillion dollars globally, it is important to understand if and how mannequins impact consumers. Are these inanimate objects, which convey society's current standard of what is beautiful with their slim legs, tiny waists and ample breasts, always beneficial for companies? Are all consumers equally affected by mannequins?

Our research shows that female mannequins' bodies essentially signal the normative standard to consumers as to what is currently perceived to be beautiful. Indeed, while female mannequins today are frequently touting a size 4 or 6, during the 1930s when food was limited mannequins more commonly fit size 18 dresses, as it was desirable to appear well fed. Our finding that female mannequins can make the normative standards of beauty salient to consumers when they display appearance-related products (e.g., a dress, bikini) is important because not all consumers respond favourably to this information. Specifically, when consumers who are low in appearance self-esteem (i.e., individuals who are not happy with their weight and/or appearance) are exposed to a female mannequin they will evaluate the product the mannequin is displaying more negatively because they are threatened by the beauty information she has made salient. Interestingly, we find that this negative response towards a female mannequin happens not only for female but also male consumers. This suggests that consumers do not compare directly to the mannequin (i.e., they do not think "Her waist is slim, while mine is not"), but rather the mannequin makes the normative standard of beauty salient and these consumers compare themselves to this more global standard (i.e., "I am not beautiful"). Finally, male mannequins do not appear to signal global standards of beauty in the same way as female mannequins; only male (but not female) consumers responded negatively when a male mannequin displayed clothing.

So, what are apparel retailers to do? If a retailers' target market is comprised of consumers low in appearance self-esteem then one solution is to decrease a female mannequin's ability to make the normative standard of beauty salient. Indeed, if the mannequin is marred (i.e., is dirty or missing her wig) or incomplete (i.e., is headless) low appearance self-esteem consumers evaluate the displayed product more favourably. In this instance, her imperfections render her as no longer an effective signal of the standard of beauty and consumers are no longer threatened. Importantly, however, if the target market consists of both low and high (i.e., individuals who are satisfied with their body/appearance) appearance self-esteem consumers, then retailers should only use headless female mannequins, as marring the mannequin decreases high appearance self-esteem consumers' evaluations of the displayed product.

TAKEAWAYS

- Avoid using a full-bodied "perfect" female mannequin if the target market is comprised of consumers who are low in appearance self-esteem.

- Using a headless mannequin will preserve product evaluations for consumers both low and high in appearance self-esteem.

REFERENCES

Argo, Jennifer J. and Darren Dahl (2017), "Signals of Beauty: The Impact of Mannequins in the Retail Context," *Journal of Consumer Research*, (forthcoming).

Dahl, Darren W., Jennifer J. Argo, and Andrea Morales (2012), "Social Information in a Retail Environment: The Importance of Referent Identity, Product Consumption, and Self-Esteem," *Journal of Consumer Research*, 38 (5), 860–871.

ENTRY #41

How can marketing make prevention education effective?

J. Craig Andrews

Professor and Kellstadt Chair in Marketing,
Marquette University

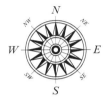

As aptly observed by Ben Franklin, "An ounce of prevention is worth a pound of cure." Today, adolescents face many risks in the form of substance abuse (e.g., prescription drugs, opioids, heroin), tobacco use, alcohol abuse, social media issues, STDs, obesity, etc., often intertwined with daily stressors, mental health challenges, and/or long-term addiction. Although the source of many of these risks can be debated, preventive education certainly trumps long-term addiction, enforcement, and lost opportunities for youth.

So, it seems that just placing preventive education campaigns, product warnings and disclosures out in the public domain would do the trick. Unfortunately, it is not that simple. Such campaign messages are destined to fail by not considering the right audience, prior beliefs, appropriate message content and imagery, and delivery modes. For example, committed non-users of tobacco can differ greatly from committed long-time users, and from those who are either open to use or have been experimenting. Our research shows that quitting thoughts for adolescent smokers exposed to graphic health warnings (GHWs) are primarily driven by evoked fear (as an emotion), whereas for young adult smokers, it is primarily due to negative health beliefs (that are more ingrained due to the young adults' longer smoking history). Even different cultures can play a role—with our research showing U.S.

adolescents experimenters to be more persuaded by the GHWs and plain tobacco packs than their counterparts in France and Spain. Before beginning campaigns, it is important to find out exactly what adolescents know, the knowledge gaps that exist, and what beliefs might best be changed.

Message content and imagery can be an issue in effectiveness as well. For instance, fear appeal themes and strength levels depend on the audience, as well as whether a solution (e.g., a hyperlink, a toll-free help line) is offered to aid self-efficacy (i.e., Can I do this myself?). Also, in the case of disclosures, such as a major adverse condition from a prescription drug, is it clearly and conspicuously displayed? That is, is it offered in visual and audio modes simultaneously, in sufficient type size, contrast, duration, and free from distractions? The right delivery modes for an adolescent audience can help with message effectiveness. For example, if the adolescent audience is primarily on certain social media sites, the campaign messages should be there as well.

Moderating conditions also matter. Our research on nutrition facts panels and symbols, and prescription drug information, shows that an audience's motivation, ability, and opportunity to process information can affect persuasion and usage. For example, low literacy or accessibility factors can affect processing of prescription drug labeling. Finally, rigorous research methodologies are essential to evaluating effectiveness, including pretesting, measure reliability and validity, the use of control groups to aid in causal inferences, targeting beliefs that can be moved, and estimating the impact on behavior with and without the campaign message in question. So, certainly, prevention education, warnings and disclosures can be effective in reducing adolescent risk taking, but only if done with some careful planning.

TAKEAWAYS

- Just because a prevention campaign or warning message is presented, does not mean that adolescents will be aware of it, comprehend it, and change their beliefs, attitudes, intentions and behavior based on it. Establishing an emotional tie and offering a viable solution (i.e., a way out) are important.

- Understanding moderating conditions can help. Adolescent motivation, ability, and opportunity to process the message and their initial beliefs matter.

- Make sure your methodology is rigorous in assessing campaign/message effectiveness. To infer that your campaign/message caused an effect, control groups often are needed.

REFERENCES

Andrews, J. Craig (2011), "Warnings and Disclosures," in Baruch Fischhoff, Noel Brewer, and Julie Downs (eds.), *Communicating Risks and Benefits: An Evidence-Based Users Guide*, Silver Spring, MD: U.S. Food & Drug Administration, 149–161.

Andrews, J. Craig, Jeremy Kees, Kala Paul, Terry Davis, and Michael Wolf (2015), "Factors to Consider in Improving Prescription Drug Pharmacy Leaflets," *International Journal of Advertising*, 34 (5), 765–788.

Andrews, J. Craig and Richard G. Netemeyer (2015), "The Role of Social Marketing in Preventing and Reducing Substance Abuse" in David Stewart (ed.), *Handbook of Persuasion and Social Marketing*, New York: Praeger, 155–194.

Andrews, J. Craig, Richard G. Netemeyer, Jeremy Kees, and Scot Burton (2014), "How Graphic Visual Health Warnings Affect Young Smokers' Thoughts of Quitting," *Journal of Marketing Research*, 51 (April), 165–183.

Andrews, J. Craig, Richard G. Netemeyer, Scot Burton, and Jeremy Kees (2016), "Effects of Plain Package Branding and Graphic Health Warnings on Adolescent Smokers in the United States, Spain, and France," *Tobacco Control*, April 18, doi:10.1136/tobaccocontrol-2015–052583.

Pechmann, Cornelia and J. Craig Andrews (2010), "Methodological Issues and Challenges in Conducting Social Impact Evaluations" in Paul N. Bloom and Edward Skloot (eds.), *Scaling Social Impact*, New York: Palgrave Macmillan, 217–234.

Walker, Matthew W. and J. Craig Andrews (2017), "The Real Cost Campaign: Evaluating Results," presentation at the 2017 Marketing & Public Policy Conference, Washington, DC, June 2.

DESTINATION #7

Motivating change

ENTRY #42

How can you influence change and innovation?

Stacy Wood

Langdon Distinguished University Chair in Marketing, Executive Director, Consumer Innovation Collaborative, Poole College of Management, North Carolina State University

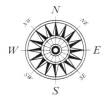

Ours is a world that constantly shouts, "New & Improved!" There are new products and services, new ways of buying things online/pop-up/mobile, new apps/wearables/devices, new sharing economies for cars/houses/clothes/etc.—so many new things. Companies desperately want to motivate consumers to try their new thing. And as consumers, we also want to motivate "new" behavior. We want to start exercise programs, change our diet, update our house, and keep up with the latest trends. We want to try the new restaurant in town and finally start organizing our finances.

What, then, is the best way to motivate people to try new things? Research shows that the answer is often not intuitive—the psychology of change is one area where we do not truly understand our own behavior. So, to be effective, we have to consider new rules of thumb and new tactics.

For example, one old adage is that people in the midst of upheaval will cling to their old favorites as a strategy for comfort. People predict that when, say, they move to a new job or town, they will be more likely to choose to eat familiar favorite foods ("comfort foods") or cling to old habits (activities, music, TV, etc.). However, this prediction turns out to be wrong. New research shows that upheaval makes us more open to new and unfamiliar things because it breaks the bonds of mindless automatic choices. In times of upheaval, old habitual cues hold less sway. So, for firms, it is interesting to know that a consumer in a new life situation (from moving to a new town to starting a family) will actually be less brand-loyal with their old favorite food or shampoo brand. And, for consumers, it is interesting to know that a new big life change, such as taking a new job, might be a great time to add other positive life changes like adding an exercise routine or quitting smoking. In other words, the new adage should be that "change begets change."

Another counterintuitive factor in change is the extent to which we let emotions color our evaluations of innovative technology. Old models held that emotions only influenced consumers' evaluations of new products in that people were happy to get product benefits and unhappy about product costs. New research, however, shows that a sizeable effect of emotion comes not from benefits/costs, but rather from the individual's initial experience with the product—when they first try it and learn how to use it. For many products, learning is not an easy process and this research shows that consumers strongly penalize products that make them feel stupid. And, sadly, this effect lasts even after the consumer has successfully learned to use the product—people do not forget that initial feeling of inadequacy. Importantly, all complex products are not doomed to suffer from this effect. Consumers' negativity stems from discrepancies between their expectations and experience. If consumers expect learning to be easy and, in reality, it is hard, the negative impact is large. But, if consumers expect learning to be hard and it is indeed hard, the negative impact is minimal. The moral of the story here is that, if you want people to change, it is critical to make that first trial or experience easy. And, if it cannot be made easy, then the important thing is to not sell it as easy, but rather to set realistic expectations.

And, finally, we do not always fully understand how our interest in change has social origins and consequences. New research suggests that empathy is key to an individual's support of social entrepreneurship and that adopting new technologies confers social benefits in being perceived as having strong leadership skills. Change may start from within, but it is a visible signal that quickly spreads to our larger interpersonal networks and, from there, to society as a whole.

TAKEAWAYS

- Times of upheaval (new move, job, family status, etc.) is a time when people are open to new brands and experiences. Change begets change.

- People do not forgive a product for making them feel stupid in the beginning. Either make the learning process easy, or set realistic expectations that it is hard.

- When we choose innovations, outsiders see us as more progressive and as better leaders.

REFERENCES

Wood, Stacy (2016), "The Psychology of Innovation," *Journal of Consumer Research*, Curation. Available at: http://jcr.oxfordjournals.org/content/psychology-innovation-summer-2016

Wood, Stacy (2012), "Prone to Progress: Using Personality to Identify Supporters of Sustainable Social Enterprise," *Journal of Public Policy and Marketing*, (Spring).

Wood, Stacy (2010), "The Comfort Food Fallacy: Avoiding Old Favorites in Times of Change," *Journal of Consumer Research*, 36 (6), 950–963.

Wood, Stacy and Steve Hoeffler (2013), "Looking Innovative: The Role of Impression Management in Use of High Tech New Products," *Journal of Product Innovation Management*, (November).

Wood, Stacy L. and C. Page Moreau (2006), "From Fear to Loathing? How Emotion Influences the Evaluation and Early Use of Innovations," *Journal of Marketing*, (July).

ENTRY #43

What role do consequences play in motivating consumers?

George Loewenstein

Herbert A. Simon Professor of Economics and Psychology, Carnegie Mellon University

Standard models of decision making are consequentialist; they assume that when people make a decision they consider the consequence of alternative courses of action, and their feelings about those consequences (utilities). When outcomes are delayed, as is usually the case, people are assumed to "discount" those consequences at a fixed discount rate; when outcomes are uncertain, people are assumed to down-weight them proportionately to their chance of happening.

Behavioral modifications of these models have generally adhered to this consequentialist perspective. For example, prospect theory assumes that people weigh probabilities, and models of hyperbolic time discounting assume that people discount probabilities, in special ways. Different models also make different assumptions about the exact form of the utility function. Prospect theory assumes that people care about gains and losses rather than overall levels of wealth; models of disappointment assume that people compare what happens to what could have happened; and models of regret assume that people compare what happens to what would have happened if they had made a different decision.

A lot of my own research has examined the consequences of immediate emotions—emotions people are experiencing at the time of decision making—as opposed to those they anticipate experiencing as a result of the decisions they make. My research on hot-cold empathy gaps shows that we have a hard time imagining how we would feel or behave in an emotional state different from the one we are in. This explains why we over-shop on an empty stomach (because when hungry, it is difficult to imagine being satiated), and why people underestimate their own risk of getting addicted (because when not craving a drug, it is almost impossible to imagine the power of craving), as well as why people who are not addicted are so intolerant of those who are. More globally, it helps to explain why we tend to make long term, often irrevocable decisions, on the basis of transient emotional states—because we cannot imagine feeling differently and assume the emotions of the moment will endure.

Immediate feelings play a key role in decision making under uncertainty, as my co-authors and I argue in a paper titled "Risk as Feelings." People take risks when it is immediately enjoyable to do so, and avoid risks that induce immediate fear. Mountain climbers and entrepreneurs are not actually especially risk-seeking, at least in other parts of their lives; they just do not find mountain climbing or business-starting scary; if anything, they find the thrill pleasurable.

Immediate feelings also play a dominant role in intertemporal choice; in neuroscience research my colleagues and I show that intertemporal choice is powerfully driven by immediate emotional influences. When it feels good to wait, as is sometimes the case for good outcomes, we actually like deferring the outcomes so we can savor the anticipation. When it feels bad to wait, as is almost always the case for unpleasant outcomes, we often prefer to get them over with quickly. Both of these patterns are easy to account for once we take account of the role of immediate emotions.

Finally, immediate feelings play a key role in the behavior of greatest interest to marketers: consumer spending. Standard models assume that when people decide whether to buy something—e.g., a cup of coffee— they are weighing the utility of that purchase against the utility of all other possible expenditures of the money—even, for example, the college tuition of one's as-yet unborn children. This is obviously unrealistic and, if it were true, would probably lead to massive overspending, since immediate consumption is so much more tangible than the delayed consumption one sacrifices for it. The reality is that people experience an immediate "pain of paying" that they weigh against the immediate pleasure of an acquisition and that brings into the present the delayed consequences of spending. People differ in the extent to which they experience such pain; tightwads experience it acutely, spendthrifts much less so. And the pain of paying depends on a wide range of situational factors that in turn influence spending—e.g., whether one is paying with cash (more pain) or credit (less); whether one is prepaying (less pain) or paying after the fact (more); whether one is paying on the margin (e.g., sushi by the piece, or cab rides in which the meter is showing) or not (e.g., a monthly bus or ski pass, or a monthly subscription to an exercise club). People who end up saving a lot, by this account, are not more far sighted; they just do not enjoy spending because the pain of paying outweighs the pleasure.

It is sometimes argued, by those who would like to differentiate humans from our nearest animal relatives, that humans are alone in their ability to contemplate, and take account of, the delayed consequences of our behavior. That may be true, but we certainly have not reached the degree of future-mindedness assumed by consequential models of decision making. Like other animals, we are very much creatures of the moment.

TAKEAWAYS

- Immediate emotions often play a significant role in decisions, we have a hard time imagining how we would feel or behave in an emotional state different from the one we are in.

- Marketers need to be aware of immediate feelings and how they contribute to consumer spending.

REFERENCES

Loewenstein, George (2001), "The Creative Destruction of Decision Research," *Journal of Consumer Research*, 24 (December), 499–505.

Keller, Punam. A., Bari Harlam, George Loewenstein, and Kevin Volpp (2011), "Enhanced Active Choice: A New Method to Motivate Behavior Change," *Journal of Consumer Psychology*, 21 (4), 376–383.

ENTRY #44

How can you enhance consumer persuasion?

Punam A. Keller

Charles Henry Jones Professor of Management, Tuck School of Business, Dartmouth College

The purpose of this essay is to demonstrate the value of segmenting consumers according to their main compliance barriers. Consumer compliance barriers typically fall into three clusters:

1. Challenges arising from a lack of Motivation or absence of meaningful value;
2. Challenges arising from a lack of Ability to make decisions; and
3. Challenges arising from difficulties in forming and following an implementation Plan.

Three projects demonstrate how persuasion can be enhanced by overcoming barriers in a 'Motivation' segment, an 'Ability' segment, and a 'Planning' segment. In each case, my field partners and I started with uncovering key barriers to assign consumers to M, A, or P segments. We then used consumer research to redesign the marketing program to overcome key compliance barriers.

PSI (Population Services International) redesigned their VMMC (voluntary medical male circumcision) for those who were not motivated to get circumcised. After identifying motivation challenges, South African males were encouraged to get circumcised by applying consumer behavioral decision solutions. For example, the depletion bias was overcome by co-opting spouses; false consensus bias (not for people who are strong, masculine, popular), was overcome via political leaders and popular entertainment stars endorsing VMMC; and present bias was reduced by offering free operation and transportation. The redesigned marketing program has resulted in more than 1 million consumers opting-in for the VMMC program. NARPP (National Association of Retired Plan Participants) redesigned Ohio State's Deferred Compensation form to increase the ability of state employees to enrol in the Sponsor's 457 retirement saving plan. The redesign was guided by consumer research on trust, vividness, and mindsets to overcome ability barriers— procrastinating, not understanding the options, inability to compute the return on investment, and confusion stemming from a lot of jargon and legal language. Consumer research on choice architecture was used to make the costs and benefits clearer and simpler in a forced choice format resulting in a 25% increase in voluntary enrolment in the Sponsor's 457 plan, as well as a 600% increase in the use of tools to increase participation rates.

Dartmouth College employees complained about several planning barriers preventing them from completing an online health and wellness assessment: ID number, confidentiality, and a change in health insurance/ insurance rates among others. Research on mindsets, implementation intentions and goal achievement was used to design a simple implementation plan containing snapshots of the first six web pages was mailed to the target audience. Each snapshot was accompanied with tips to overcoming each implementation challenge. For example, ID challenges were overcome with options to use a social security number. Another web-page shot reassured consumers that the assessment would not affect their ability to get health insurance now or in the future or cause an increase/cancellation of their current insurance plan. This simple six-step plan resulted in a 93.3% increase in completion.

The M-A-P segmentation approach can be used to enhance consumer engagement, empowerment, and compliance by addressing key consumer challenges.

TAKEAWAYS

- Insights on compliance barriers is key to increasing compliance.
- Segment the target audience by key compliance barriers— motivation, ability, or planning barriers.
- Consumer research provides effective solutions for overcoming specific compliance barriers.

REFERENCES

Keller, Punam A. (2015), "Social Marketing and Healthy Behaviors," in David W. Stewart (ed.), *Handbook of Persuasion and Social Marketing*, Chapter 2, New York: Routledge, 9–38.

Keller, Punam A., Bari Harlam, George Loewenstein, and Kevin Volpp (2011), "Enhanced Active Choice: A New Method to Motivate Behavior Change," *Journal of Consumer Psychology*, 21 (4), 376–383.

Keller, Punam A. and Annamaria Lusardi (2010), "Employee Retirement Savings: What We Know and What We are Discovering for Helping People to Prepare for Life After Work," in David Mick, Simone Pettigrew, Connie Pechmann, and Julie Ozanne (eds.), *Transformative Consumer Research for Personal and Collective Well Being: Reviews and Frontiers*, New York: Taylor & Francis, 445–464.

Scammon, Debra, Punam A. Keller, et al. (2011), "Transforming Consumer Health," *Journal of Public Policy and Marketing*, 30 (1), 14–22.

ENTRY #45

How can you use negative associations to motivate consumers?

Katherine White

Professor, Marketing and Behavioral Science, Sauder School of Business, University of British Columbia

Marketers often use the notion of "reference groups" to create positive associations with the products they wish to promote. The term reference group refers to those groups or group members who can influence consumers' attitudes and behaviors. While marketers commonly link the brand to reference groups that are inclusive or aspirational in nature (i.e., membership and aspirational reference groups, respectively), we show that the motivation to avoid the negative association of a group or an individual can have implications for consumer behavior. We refer to these types of groups as "dissociative" reference groups. Dissociative reference groups are those groups with whom individuals wish to avoid being associated with and thereby "disidentify" with them. Take for example, the millennial that does not want their new pair of sneakers to be associated with being "uncool," the baby boomer wants to avoid being seen as "elderly," and the man who does not want to wear a shirt that makes him look "feminine."

Our work shows that consumers will avoid dissociative options and choose alternative options in order to do so. For example, males had more negative evaluations of, and were less inclined to choose, a product associated with a dissociative (i.e., female) reference group than a neutral product. Simply giving one of the options a dissociative label—the ladies' cut steak—led men to avoid this product and instead choose an alternative option with a neutral association (White and Dahl 2006). This effect was heightened when the product was to be consumed in front of others and among consumers who were focused on the public self-image that they conveyed to others. Furthermore, dissociative influence is heightened when the consumers own membership group identity is particularly salient (White and Dahl 2007). Interestingly, the dissociative effect can be a more compelling motivator than the desire to associate with an in-group. Marketers can successfully promote a brand or focal option by associating the alternative option (such as a competitor's product) with a dissociative reference group. Think of the classic Apple vs. PC ads, where the PC is associated with an outdated, older, and dowdy referent in the hopes that consumer will opt for the cooler, hipper alternative—the Mac.

While most of our work demonstrates that people will avoid products and behaviors that are endorsed by dissociative reference groups, we also find an exception to this rule. Sometimes consumers will exhibit similar behaviors to dissociative reference groups (White, Simpson, and Argo 2013). In particular, when a consumer learns that a dissociative out-group performs comparatively well on a positively viewed behavior (such as composting), and the context is very public in nature, the consumer is more likely to respond with similar actions. This is because learning of the successful performance of a dissociative out-group under public conditions threatens the consumer's group image and activates the desire to present the group image in a positive light. Providing information regarding the comparatively positive actions of a dissociative out-group may be an effective behavior-change strategy when a consumer's behavior is likely to be publicly viewed by others.

TAKEAWAYS

- Including a dissociative option in a decision set can steer consumer decisions to an alternative option.

- Use dissociative influence in situations that are public. Consumers are particularly motivated to avoid the negative implications of dissociative groups when the context is public in nature.

- Motivate positive behaviors and actions by highlighting the positive actions of dissociative groups.

REFERENCES

Dunn, Lea, Katherine White, and Darren W. Dahl (2012), "That is So Not Me: Dissociating from Undesired Consumer Identities", in Russell Belk and Ayalla Ruvio (eds.), *Identity and Consumption*, Routledge.

White, Katherine and Darren W. Dahl (2006), "To Be or Not Be: The Influence of Dissociative Reference Groups on Consumer Preferences," *Journal of Consumer Psychology*, 16 (4), 404–414.

White, Katherine and Darren W. Dahl (2007), "Are all Outgroups Created Equal? Consumer Identity and Dissociative Influence," *Journal of Consumer Research*, 34 (4), 525–536.

White, Katherine, Bonnie Simpson, and Jennifer J. Argo (2014), "The Motivating Role of Dissociative Outgroups in Encouraging Positive Consumer Behaviors," *Journal of Marketing Research*, 51 (4), 433–447.

ENTRY #46

How can you tap into consumers' surroundings to influence their actions?

Juliano Laran
Professor of Marketing, University of Miami School of Business Administration

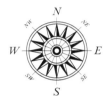

Consumers pursue goals throughout the course of each day. Consider the act of choosing what to eat for lunch, whether to buy an expensive or cheaper outfit, or what to do on a Thursday evening. We pick something healthy (vs. tasty) because we have the goal of maintaining or losing weight, buy an expensive (vs. cheaper) outfit because we have the goal of impressing others, go out with friends (vs. stay late at work) because we have the goal to have fun.

While we may have some of these goals in life, many times we do things that are inconsistent with our life goals. Buying an expensive outfit may serve a sudden urge to impress others, but may also represent going beyond our budget and incurring debt. How is this possible when we have a life goal of always having enough money to pay for our bills? The research I have conducted with my colleagues shows that many times our immediate environment makes certain goals momentarily salient, and we pursue these goals even though they are not goals that we generally hold in life.

We found that when people are exposed to information that makes them feel like we live in a harsh world, with scarcity of resources, they tend to immediately prefer high calorie foods. People ate more food that was described as being "high calorie" when they saw information about struggle and adversity, something that did not happen with low calorie food. This means that even though people understand that they should control their calorie intake, they eat more calories, and actually do not want low calorie food, when they are exposed to information suggesting we live in a harsh world. Importantly, when asked people did not show any awareness that they had been exposed to such information, meaning that they ate more high calorie food without knowing what made them want to do it. Similar effects were found in the context of spending, as people spent more money when exposed to information in their environment about spending without their awareness.

Fortunately, people can also benefit from the influence of information in their surrounding environment. We found that when people are exposed to information about making careful choices they tend to pick healthy food items most of the times, such as choosing a granola bar vs. potato chips, even though they are not aware of the information. This occurs because the information makes them focus on what can be good for them and ignore food items that can be harmful. We also found that when people are exposed to slogans in the marketplace suggesting they should spend money (e.g., "Luxury, you deserve it.", "Because you can afford it.") they actually prefer to save, spending less of their money. This occurs because with practice people can develop a mechanism that helps them understand that certain marketplace agents are there to persuade them, and they defend themselves against this persuasion by doing the opposite of what has been suggested.

This perspective of the influence of the environment on people's behavior without their awareness suggests that people should engineer their environment in a way that conduces to better choices. This means avoiding information about harshness and spending, and surrounding oneself with information about abundance and being careful. Fortunately, we learn overtime, and if people understand and consistently bring to mind thoughts about how the environment can make them perform harmful behaviors they will eventually learn how to defend themselves.

TAKEAWAYS

- Consumers are sensitive to the information in their environment, which means they can be influenced without their awareness.

- Consider which tools will be used to steer consumers in a certain direction as they have developed mechanisms to defend themselves against wanted influence.

- It is important to understand the goals consumers have as trying to steer them toward pursuing goals that they already have could benefit both companies and consumers.

REFERENCES

Laran, Juliano, Amy Dalton, and Eduardo Andrade (2011), "The Curious Case of Behavioral Backlash: Why Brands Produce Priming Effects and Slogans Produce Reverse Priming Effects," *Journal of Consumer Research*, 37 (April), 999–1014.

Laran, Juliano and Anthony Salerno (2013), "Life History Strategy, Food Choice, and Caloric Consumption," *Psychological Science*, 24 (February), 167–173.

Laran, Juliano, Chris Janiszewski, and Anthony Salerno (2016), "Exploring the Differences between Conscious and Unconscious Goal Pursuit," *Journal of Marketing Research*, 53 (June), 442–458.

ENTRY #47

Does consumers' phototaking enrich or impoverish experience?

Gal Zauberman

Professor of Marketing, Yale School of Management

Kristin Diehl

Associate Professor of Marketing, Marshall School of Business, University of Southern California

Alix Barasch

Assistant Professor of Marketing, Stern School of Business, New York University

Experiences make up some of the most important aspects of our lives. From traveling to a new city to having a cup of coffee at your favorite coffee shop, nowadays these experiences often involve taking photos, to the tune of an estimated 1.2 trillion pictures in 2017 alone. We take these photos to capture memories for ourselves or so we can share moments with others. Companies often encourage photo-sharing to generate word of mouth. However, given the time and importance phototaking occupies in our lives, it is baffling how little we know about how photo-taking affects the very experiences we capture.

In several research projects involving experiments with thousands of respondents engaging in a variety of activities (e.g., taking a bus tour, eating in a food court), both in the lab and in the field, we began answering the question: how does photo-taking affect our immediate enjoyment and long-term memories of experiences?

One can often hear others say that taking photos ruins experiences, and that people should put down their cameras and just live in the moment. However, that is not what we find when studying this question empirically. In fact, we find that taking photos actually increases enjoyment with the experience, relative to not taking photos. When people take photos, they report feeling more engaged and they look longer and more frequently at aspects of interest in the experience, providing further behavioral evidence for the engagement process. This heightened engagement intensifies the experience, which makes positive experiences better (leading to greater enjoyment from photo-taking), but also makes negative experiences even worse.

Of course, there are always situations where photo-taking becomes less beneficial, even for positive experiences. For example, when one is already actively engaged in an experience (e.g., participating in an arts demonstration instead of just watching it), photo-taking does not heighten engagement and enjoyment. Also, when photo-taking becomes cumbersome (e.g., using bulky camera equipment), photo-taking loses its advantages. Further, what one plans to do with these photos also matters. We find that taking photos with the goal of sharing them with others does not increase engagement and enjoyment as much as taking photos for oneself. When people take photos to share (e.g., on social media), they, during the experience, consider how those photos will be viewed and evaluated by others, causing them to feel self-presentational concern and reducing their enjoyment of the experience.

People also often take photos to capture moments for posterity, not just for immediate enjoyment. We find that photo-taking also affects what people remember, even without looking back at the photos themselves. For example, during a museum visit, people may view various artifacts, paintings, and displays while also listening to an audio guide explaining what they are looking at. Photo-taking focuses attention on the visual aspects at the expense of the auditory aspects; hence, when people take photos, they remember more of what they see, but less of what they hear.

In sum, photo-taking is playing an increasingly important and prevalent role in our lives. More research like this is necessary to understand its impact on consumers, not just in the short run, but also in the long run.

TAKEAWAYS

- Encourage photo-taking for positive experiences, particularly when experiences are not highly engaging.

- Facilitate photo-taking that does not interfere with the experience (e.g., create set-ups where neither flash nor bulky camera equipment are needed).

- Discourage photo-taking for negative experiences.

- During the experience, encourage photo-taking for one's own memories, rather than to share broadly on social media.

- Encourage photo-taking when visual information is important to remember, and discourage photo-taking when auditory information is important to remember.

REFERENCES

Barasch, Alixandra, Kristin Diehl, Jackie Silverman, and Gal Zauberman, "Photographic Memory: The Effects of Volitional Photo-Taking on Remembering Visual and Auditory Aspects of an Experience," *Psychological Science*, 28 (8), 1056–1066.

Barasch, Alixandra, Gal Zauberman, and Kristin Diehl, "How the Intention to Share Can Undermine Enjoyment: Photo-taking Goals and Evaluation of Experiences," working paper.

Diehl, Kristin, Gal Zauberman, and Alixandra Barasch (2016), "How Taking Photos Increases the Enjoyment of Experiences," *Journal of Personality and Social Psychology*, 111 (2), (August), 119–140.

ENTRY #48

What can you do to stay motivated throughout your career?

Brian Wansink

John S. Dyson Professor of Marketing, Cornell University

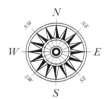

The happiest and most productive academic in the universe is one you have never heard of. I met him 25 years ago when a New Hampshire blizzard snowed us into a small convention hotel we were speaking at. I suggested we get dinner.

He was about 50 and extraordinarily outgoing and fun and almost seemed to have a glow around him. He was a tenured at a nearby state college, and I was a research-obsessed untenured professor at Dartmouth.

Being research obsessed, once we settled down for dinner I asked him about his research interests and he said, "Ski resorts." As I scanned my brain for academic literature on ski resorts, he tried again, "I study ski resorts and marketing."

"Uh, only that?" I asked.

"Yep, only that. I love to ski and that is all I study. I look at how people decide which resort to go to, what can make them satisfied if the weather's bad, or whether they should buy a day pass or a season pass. All theories are relevant for skiers or ski resorts," he enthusiastically declared.

Like most researchers, I had been trained to believe Theory was King. More specifically, general theories are king, not ski resort theories.

My new friend had a different view. He focused his entire career on solving problems for ski resorts in an academic way. He published three or four papers a year, spoke at conventions, took his family on consulting trips to Switzerland, was on ski resort boards around the world, and taught college electives on ski resort-related things. His college loved him, his students loved him, his family loved him, and ski resorts really, really loved him. From everything I could see in our two days together, he was about the happiest and most productive academic I had known. He was the greatest academic in the universe—in the ski resort universe.

Academia let us choose to become the greatest academic in our universe. But many people do not do this. They do not specify an important universe that excites them. Some might do a dissertation on what their adviser says is "hot," but then become disenchanted after graduation. Others might, as I overheard one associate professor say, "Crank up the B— S— Machine," until they get tenure and then "play the publishing game" after that.

When people ask for academic strategies for success, they expect to hear, "Publish six or more A-level papers before tenure." That may work for the Olympic-level scholars, but not for the other 95% of us. Instead, I think the best strategy for success is simply, "Keep your fire burning." Find the domain you want to change—either because of an emotional connection, for justice reasons, or because it is your lifelong passion. If you can stay motivated and hopeful through your career, you will be a success regardless of whatever unexpected things might happen.

My new friend had found a way to keep his fire burning for years after his Ph.D. program. It was a fireplace in a ski lodge, and it made a lot of people very, very happy.

TAKEAWAYS

- Keep the fire burning.

- Find a domain you want to change because of an emotional connection, for justice reasons, or because it is your lifelong passion.

- If you can stay motivated and hopeful through your career, you will be a success regardless of whatever unexpected things might happen.

- Be the greatest academic in your universe.

- The ski resort universe is already taken.

REFERENCES

Wansink, Brian (2014), *Slim by Design – Mindless Eating Solutions for Everyday Life*, New York: William Morrow.

Wansink, Brian (2011), "Activism Research: Designing Research that Intends to Transform," in David Mick, Simone Pettigrew, Connie Pechmann, and Julie Ozanne (eds.), *Transformative Consumer Research for Personal and Collective Well-Being*, New York: Routledge, 67–88.

Wansink, Brian (2006), *Mindless Eating – Why We Eat More Than We Think*, New York: Bantam-Dell.

Wansink, Brian (2005), *Marketing Nutrition – Soy, Functional Foods, Biotechnology, and Obesity*, Champaign, IL: University of Illinois Press.

DESTINATION #8

Marketing and the world at large

ENTRY #49

What does wisdom entail and how can it make you a better marketer?

David Glen Mick

Robert Hill Carter Professor of Commerce, McIntire School of Commerce, University of Virginia

Wisdom has been virtually non-existent in the field of marketing. Perhaps it has seemed irrelevant, yet wisdom has been called the apex of human qualities. Perhaps it seems intractable, yet related research has intensified in the social sciences during the last 30 years.

In the same timeframe, consumers have been increasingly characterized as unreflective and flawed (e.g., myopic, overconfident, pawn to emotions). Implicitly or explicitly, marketing executives have been frequently portrayed in similar ways, in addition to a lack of rectitude and a sole immediate focus on ROI and market-share.

Wisdom—the opposite of foolishness—is the application of knowledge in pursuit of well-being and the common good. It involves balancing intrapersonal, interpersonal, and extrapersonal factors in the context of short- and long-term horizons. Pillars of wisdom include recognizing and dealing with pervasive uncertainty, engaging regularly in moral reasoning, distinguishing and managing emotions, demonstrating consistent compassion and gratitude, learning sincerely from mistakes, and nurturing patience and resilience. It is ultimately a transcendent and meta-functional mental quality that is realized as mindfulness of one's motives, thoughts, feelings, and tendencies in the process of judging, deciding, and taking actions.

That all sounds impossibly Godly. But not necessarily. In one study of consumer choices, those rated wiser exhibited evidence of strong personal intentions, prudent deliberation, and a clear linkage from values and knowledge to action, each of which the wisdom literature features. New research on nutrition has also showed that wisdom through mindfulness can inhibit consumption of unhealthy foods. And in the workaday world, one study showed that executives revered for their wise leadership were described in detailed stories as being more humble, more forbearing, more accountable, and less egocentric. It is discouraging that our professional associations are not leading more honorably in these regards.

Naturally, not every decision can evoke wisdom in its fuller forms. In our warp-speed, information-avalanched world, it is often necessary to simply satisfice or take shortcuts. But even these tactics have their better and worse manifestations, depending on the outcomes for well-being. Ditto for habits.

Can wisdom be taught or encouraged? Many researchers say yes. Students in high school or in university business programs can engage with complex cases, moral dilemmas, and everyday problems in which they are tasked with applying wisdom components for deriving more constructive and uplifting solutions. Websites and computer apps can remind consumers and executives to slow down, rise above, confront emotions, contemplate values, curtail egos, and strive on for a more flourishing life.

TAKEAWAYS

- Assume that consumers aspire to be well across multiple dimensions of life (e.g., physically, emotionally, socially, financially, environmentally) and they can be guided by educators, businesses, and policy makers to achieve this goal through wiser living.

- Assume that most people in executive and managerial positions want to do what is wise as much as possible—not just for themselves, business owners, and stockholders, but also for consumers, employees, and the environment overall.

- Wisdom research can be culled, communicated, and encouraged across all of life's dimensions.

REFERENCES

Bahl, Shalini, George R. Milne, Spencer M. Ross, David Glen Mick, Sonya A. Grier, Sunaina K. Chugani, Steven Chan, Stephen J. Gould, Joshua D. Dorsey, Yoon-Na Cho, Robert M. Schindler, Sabine Boesen Mariani, and Mitchel R. Murdock (2016), "Mindfulness: The Transformative Potential for Consumer, Societal, and Environmental Well-Being," *Journal of Public Policy and Marketing*, 35 (2), 198–210.

Fournier, Susan, Susan Dobscha, and David Glen Mick (1998), "Preventing the Premature Death of Relationship Marketing," *Harvard Business Review*, January–February, 42–51.

Mick, David Glen (2007), "The End(s) of Marketing and the Neglect of Moral Responsibility by the American Marketing Association," *Journal of Public Policy and Marketing*, 26 (2), 289–292.

Mick, David Glen, Thomas S. Bateman, and Richard J. Lutz (2009), "Wisdom: Exploring the Pinnacle of Human Virtues as a Central Link from Micromarketing to Macromarketing," *Journal of Macromarketing*, 29 (2), 98–118.

Mick, David Glen and Barry Schwartz (2012), "Can Consumers Be Wise? Aristotle Speaks to the 21st Century," in David Glen Mick, Simone Pettigrew, Cornelia Pechmann, and Julie L. Ozanne (eds.), *Transformative Consumer Research for Personal and Collective Well-Being*, New York: Taylor and Francis/Routledge, 663–680.

The University of Chicago's Center for Practical Wisdom: http://wisdomresearch. org/

The Wisdom Page: www.wisdompage.com/index.html

ENTRY #50

How is collaboration beneficial to you and your business?

Julie L. Ozanne
Professor of Marketing, University of Melbourne

Lucie K. Ozanne
Associate Professor of Marketing, University of Canterbury

Disasters are something that happens to someone else, right? Think again. As the world heats up, disasters are becoming increasingly common worldwide.

We know that collaborative forms of consumption are on the rise too—from toy libraries, tool sharing, and co-housing to couch surfing, garden sharing, and local exchange trading systems. These peer-to-peer networks allow members to give and receive goods and services. But how can they help you during a time of crisis?

During the 2011 Christchurch earthquakes, one peer-to-peer network —a time bank—helped the town of Lyttelton survive the immediate devastation and assisted in the years of rebuilding the town. For people who could not return to their homes, the time bank found shelter. For housebound elderly, they arranged for neighbors to stop by offering food and solace. For homes buried in rubble, they organized teams of helpers to dig out neighbors. The time bank provided a constant flow of critical and timely information. This assistance involved hundreds of hours of help that spanned months and years. But during a disaster, the very fabric of social life comes apart. How is it possible that a local exchange network was so resilient?

Years before the ground began to shake, neighbors were swapping their favorite skills with their neighbors. This swapping was facilitated by having a time bank coordinator match traders. When you traded one hour of your labor, you received an hour of time credit—a time bank hour. You could then use this time bank hour to purchase someone else's labor. Importantly, this was an egalitarian network where everyone's skills were equally valued and people were committed.

During the years before the earthquake struck, hundreds of people traded thousands of hours. In doing so, they were building a social network made up of weak and strong ties. These face-to-face trades were sometime utilitarian but often services were given in compassion and for mutual benefits, such as when a neighbor was sick, the local school needed help, or the community garden needed attention.

It is important that this was a local network—disasters are local events and first responders are often your family and neighbors. Moreover, the time bank was building an opportunity network that was practiced. For months in the lead up to the crisis, the network was tackling bigger problems. These group projects were high in task jointness, meaning people must interact, adjust, and coordinate their activities to achieve a common goal; as task jointness increases, so too does group commitment and cohesion. But they were also having fun as members came together to clean up beaches, throw street parties, and provide educational classes.

Prior to the earthquake, the time bank had created a rich social network composed of diverse ties through which a variety of resources flowed. As such, the time bank was well practiced at assembling different members to solve problems, and then disassembling—again and again, again and again. Thus, when disaster struck, the time bank was the only local organization that was practiced at identifying and mobilizing townspeople with a wide variety of skills.

This type of response is not unusual. At the time of the earthquake, universities closed down. Students using social media spontaneously formed a volunteer army to come to the aid of their neighbors; this idea of compassionate giving is spreading globally (www.sva.org.nz/). Although these were local responses, these new models of exchange can spread quickly through social media. Might collaborative consumption one day say your life? Only time will tell, but its promise lies in creating diverse networks that bind people together even across their differences.

TAKEAWAYS

- Get involved in your local community in face-to-face exchanges with your neighbors; join a toy library, participate in a neighborhood tool library, start a time bank, or work on a community project together.

- Create an egalitarian network where all members can participate and that is guided by participatory democracy where people feel their voice matters. As long as people are coming together trading, they are building the network.

- Nobody can practice weekly for the capacities needed in a disaster. But if you are exchanging and having fun, then you are creating a network animated by joy and fostering connections that make a community more resilient.

REFERENCES

Cahn, Edgar S. (2004), *No More Throw Away People: The Co-Production Imperative*, Washington, DC: Essential Books.

Ozanne, Lucie K. (2016), TedxChristchurch, "A Secret Weapon for True Disaster Resilience." Available at: www.youtube.com/watch?v=iQxryNvZnbI

Ozanne, Lucie K. and Julie L. Ozanne (2016), "How Alternative Consumer Markets Can Build Community Resiliency," *European Journal of Marketing*, 50 (3/4), 330–357.

Ozanne, Lucie K. and Julie L. Ozanne (2011), "A Child's Right to Play: The Social Construction of Civic Virtues in Toy Libraries," *Journal of Public Policy & Marketing*, Fall, 30 (2), 263–276.

Phipps, Marcus and Julie L. Ozanne (2017), "Routines Disrupted: Reestablishing Security through Practice Alignment," *Journal of Consumer Research*, 44, (2), 361–380.

ENTRY #51

How can you employ macromarketing to better your business?

Clifford J. Shultz, II

Charles H. Kellstadt Professor of Marketing, International Fellow, Harvard-Fulbright Economics Teaching Program

The fundamental purpose of marketing is to sustain societies, and to enhance the well-being of communities and people. We seem to have lost sight of that, at our peril. So, let us go forward boldly and re-focus marketing to save the world. Considerations for that mission follow.

Soon after Homo Sapiens climbed from the primal ooze, agreed to cooperate, formed tribes, and began to advance civilization, exchange—and eventually, systemic marketing exchange—was indispensable to survival. To save the world as humans knew it—as we desired it to be—we had to engage in marketing. Tribes grew to communities, to villages, to nation states and trade blocs; markets and marketing were instrumental to health, wealth and well-being. The existence of more than seven billion people on Marketsphere Earth is compelling evidence that marketing institutions and initiatives do facilitate human survival; especially when we consider that nearly every country on earth is now administered by some form of market(ing)-based economy. Truly, well-regulated markets and ethical marketing practices enable people, communities, societies, and countries to thrive.

Yet, for all the successes of Homo Sapiens cum Homo Marketus, our fragile biosphere is being ravaged by war and violence; human exploitation and disenfranchisement; excessive harvesting, extraction, pollution and other devastations. These assaults are exacerbated by voracious consumer demands and short-sighted, dubious policies and businesses practices; including goods, services, behaviors and outcomes derived from marketing. The scale and scope of the assaults increasingly are an existential threat to every living thing on Earth. Thus, we find ourselves in a complex, planet-wide commons dilemma, greatly driven by irresponsible, myopic consumption, markets and marketing, which may offer short-term gains for some, but at unacceptable long-term costs to all. Marketing giveth; marketing taketh away.

The tragedy of our global-marketing-commons is that most marketing practitioners and scholars, while not necessarily oblivious to the threat, are not sufficiently committed to marketing as a form of constructive engagement to ameliorate or to reverse the tragedy. We give lip-service to "sustainability" and "society at large," but actions suggest most marketers, marketing firms and marketing scholars are more concerned with, and rewarded for, shorter-term goals. We therefore must re-emphasize marketing as a systemic endeavor; a provisioning agent and societal function to enhance the human condition.

Toward that macromarketing agenda let us (re)consider marketing as a form of constructive engagement for creating, communicating, pricing and delivering goods, services and experiences to consumers and organizations in complex, interacting systems; for the purpose of managing consumer, societal, economic, and political relationships in ways that benefit local, regional, and global stakeholders, inclusively, equitably, and sustainably. Indeed, commons-friendly marketing communications, products and practices, appropriate pricing, new marketing experiences and so forth—in coordination with good governance of our complex and often conflicted communities, countries and planet—are imperative.

If marketers and the marketing academy embrace macromarketing—and focus on the study and management of complex systems, to enhance the sustainable well-being of people, communities, societies and our biosphere—we can be the vanguard of a movement, saving ourselves from oblivion, as marketing saves the world.

TAKEAWAYS

- Think, plan and act, systemically, spatially and temporally—from design to disposal of any product, service, experience or policy.

- Map the forces, players and relationships in the marketing system in which you function or aspire to function: where are problems/opportunities; where do or might conflicts arise; how might policies and the marketing mix mitigate or eliminate those conflicts; how will your engagement ensure sustainable and equitable goals, via changes in marketing activities and consumer behaviors?

- Adopt rewards and incentive-structures that affect sustainable, multi-win outcomes for as many stakeholders as possible, locally and globally.

- Do well by doing good: be sure to address and manage the needs of key decision makers and the most vulnerable; find a way to do this, profitably—or perhaps just any part of it, profitably—and the world will beat a path to your door.

- Carpe diem.

REFERENCES

Barrios, Andres, Kristina De Valck, Clifford Shultz, Olivier Sibai, Katharina Husemann, Matthew Maxwell-Smith, and Marius Luedicke (2016), "Marketing as a Means to Transformative Social Conflict Resolution: Lessons from Transitioning War Economies and the Colombian Coffee Marketing System," *Journal of Public Policy & Marketing*, 35 (2), 185–197.

Manfredo, Mark and Clifford Shultz (2007), "Risk, Trade, Recovery and the Consideration of Real Options: The Imperative Coordination of Policy, Marketing, and Finance in the Wake of Catastrophe," *Journal of Public Policy & Marketing*, 26 (1), 33–48.

Mittelstaedt, John, Clifford Shultz, William Kilbourne, and Mark Peterson (2014), "Sustainability as Megatrend: Two Schools of Macromarketing Thought," *Journal of Macromarketing*, 34 (3), 253–264.

Shultz, Clifford (2016), "Marketing an End to War: Constructive Engagement, Community Wellbeing, and Sustainable Peace," *Markets, Globalization & Development Review*, 1 (2), Article 2, 1–23. Available at: http://digitalcommons.uri.edu/cgi/viewcontent.cgi?article=1015&context=mgdr

Shultz, Clifford (2015), "The Ethical Imperative of Constructive Engagement in a World Confounded by the Commons Dilemma, Social Traps, and Geo-political Conflicts," in Alexander Nill (ed.), *Handbook on Ethics in Marketing*, Northampton, MA: Edward Elgar, 188–219.

Shultz, Clifford (1997), "Improving Life Quality for the Destitute: Contributions from Multiple-Method Fieldwork in War-Ravaged Transition Economies," *Journal of Macromarketing*, 17 (1), 56–67.

Shultz, Clifford and Morris Holbrook (2009), "The Paradoxical Relationship between Marketing and Vulnerability," *Journal of Public Policy & Marketing*, 28 (1), 124–127.

Shultz, Clifford and Morris Holbrook (1999), "Marketing and the Tragedy of the Commons: A Synthesis, Commentary, and Analysis for Action," *Journal of Public Policy & Marketing*, 18 (2), 218–229.

ENTRY #52

How is sustainability changing the marketing world?

C. B. Bhattacharya

Zoffer Chair of Sustainability and Ethics, Katz Graduate School of Business, University of Pittsburgh

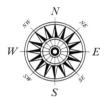

I met "Ben" of Ben & Jerry's at a leadership conference in Atlanta in 1994; he was also interested in consumer behavior, if on a less granular level. "You know, there is something that intrigues me," he said at some point in our conversation. "We do a lot for the environment and we do a lot for society. Can you help me understand if what we do for the environment and society . . . does it help us sell ice cream? Do consumers care enough about this stuff to influence their purchase decision?" I do not know the answer, I said, but I was intrigued. Ben Cohen was talking about an outcome, "sales," which marketing scholars and business in general cared about a lot. But he was also talking about environmental and social attributes as drivers of sales, which marketing scholars were not thinking of in any rigorous, systematic way.

Thus began an important chapter of my professional life—uncovering the "business case" for investing in corporate responsibility and sustainability initiatives. I had the opportunity to study this question of stakeholder reactions to sustainability from various angles and had the privilege of working with several companies—including Procter and Gamble, General Mills, Eli Lilly, Timberland, Green Mountain Coffee, Stonyfield Farm and others in depth—and published many articles showing that, under certain conditions, stakeholders such as consumers and employees do reward companies for their sustainability initiatives.

As explicated in my 2011 book co-authored with Sankar Sen and Daniel Korschun, "Leveraging Corporate Responsibility: The Stakeholder Route to Maximizing Business and Social Value," stakeholder reactions can be distilled into three main factors: Understanding, Usefulness, and Unity, which we also call the 3 Us framework. Understanding constitutes the first step where stakeholders assess whether sustainability programs are in fact improving societal welfare and try to uncover what motivated the company to engage in sustainability in the first place. The second aspect of stakeholder interpretation of sustainability is Usefulness, or the degree to which the activities provide some form of functional or psycho-social benefit to the stakeholder. Finally, Unity is "identification" or the overall sense that the company's values match those of the stakeholder—the mediator that drives the value that companies seek from sustainability investments. Our results indicate that if management is seen to fully back a company's regard for people and planet alongside profit, employees become more engaged and loyal, which not only results in lower employee turnover, but is also recognized by customers. This latter group, in turn, identifies more with the company and its products and services, raising revenues.

Of late, I have been looking into what companies need to do to shift sustainability issues to the core of their thinking and practice. I started by creating a Sustainable Business Roundtable at ESMT, a peer-to-peer learning network for leading companies interested in conducting business "through the sustainability lens." In parallel, I have spent a lot of time on the front lines of the corporate world interviewing dozens of top-flight executives and scores of hardy employees, from middle managers to workers on the shop floor to better understand best practices and road-blocks.

My experiences in the classroom, the boardroom, the mid-level office, and the factory floor form the bedrock of my future research. In a world where environmental and societal challenges pose a real threat to our very existence and stakeholders are becoming more and more vocal about it, embedding sustainability into the corporate DNA is a business imperative.

TAKEAWAYS

- Companies need to eschew the notion that sustainability must be enacted in a top-down way. Stakeholders want to be the enactors of sustainability, with the company serving mainly as an enabler and source of aggregation of corporate resources.

- Communication needs to become more prominent in sustainability planning. Too many companies limit their sustainability communication to an annual report and a few electronic repositories. Sustainability management needs to include a communication plan that clearly articulates how effective programs are, how they fit into the company's strategic plan and how sustainability can benefit stakeholders.

- Companies that want to maximize sustainability value are going to have to measure stakeholder responses with more discipline than they currently do. Only a few companies effectively measure the value generated by sustainability activities.

REFERENCES

Bhattacharya, C.B., Sankar Sen, and Daniel Korschun (2011), "Leveraging corporate responsibility: The stakeholder route to maximizing business and social value," Cambridge, UK: Cambridge University Press.

Bhattacharya, C.B. and Paul Polman (2017), "Sustainability Lessons From the Front Lines," *MIT Sloan Management Review*, 58 (2), 71.

Du, Shuili, C.B. Bhattacharya, and Sankar Sen (2011), "Corporate Social Responsibility and Competitive Advantage: Overcoming the Trust Barrier," *Management Science*, 57 (9), 1528–1545.

Luo, Xueming and Bhattacharya, C.B. (2006), "Corporate social responsibility, customer satisfaction, and market value," *Journal of Marketing*, 70 (4), 1–18.

ENTRY #53

How does climate determine consumption and culture?

Jagdish Sheth

Charles H. Kellstadt Professor of Marketing,
Goizueta Business School, Emory University

Everyone knows that there are differences across cultures in our consumption of necessities such as food, shelter, and clothing. However, we do not know why these differences persist despite globalization. In a recent book I published, *Genes, Climate and Consumption Culture: Connecting the Dots* (Emerald Publishing, 2017), I document that consumption as well as cultural differences such as individualism, punctuality, and territorialism are due to the North–South differences in climate ranging from the arctic to temperate to tropical climates.

My interest in climate grew out of a research study we were doing for Coca Cola International. Coca Cola consumption varied enormously from country to country. It was as low as 64 bottles per year per capita in one country and as high as 400 bottles per year per capita in other countries. Given that this was an empirical observation, a large-scale correlation analysis revealed that more than 95% of the variance can be explained by two factors: climate of the country and age of the population. Warmer countries with young populations consumed more Coca Cola and vice-versa. The highest per capita consumption was in Mexico (400 bottles) and the lowest per capita consumption was in Sweden (64 bottles). Furthermore, the country's climate was twice as important as the age of its inhabitants.

Climate is the root cause of who we are genetically, how we behave culturally, and how we behave as consumers of three basic necessities common to all civilizations: food, shelter, and clothing.

The best way to illustrate consumption differences in food, shelter, and clothing is to contrast Northern and Southern Europeans. In the North above the Alps, the source of protein, calories, and fat is animal because of the lack of vegetation. Therefore, the Northern European diet tends to be what we refer to as meat and potatoes. In contrast, the Mediterranean cultures have more lentils, vegetables, nuts and fruits in their diet because they can grow them. The Northern European diet tends to be less spicy, whereas tropical countries such as India have an enormous variety of spices. In my research on cheese consumption, I was surprised to discover that the fat content of cheese (Swiss) in cold climates is very high (40% or more); it drops to low-fat content (2 to 3%) in the Mediterranean temperate climate (feta and mozzarella); and the concept of cheese is conspicuously absent in tropical climates. For inhabitants of tropical climates, saturated fat comes from olive oil, coconut oil, and avocado, for example.

Northern Europeans depend on animals for clothing materials and, therefore, their preference is for wool and leather. Whereas, warmer climate cultures have access to cotton and linen. Northern Europeans prefer multiple layers and tight-fitting clothes to create insulation, but in warmer climates loose, single-layer, free-flowing garments that provide ventilation are more prevalent. Given that vegetation is not possible in Northern Europe, the preference is for pastel colors in clothes. On the other hand, warmer climates prefer a colorful display of clothing, as exemplified by Indian Saris, native African garments, and colorful Pacific Island outfits. Finally, boots are replaced with shoes, shoes are replaced with sandals, and sandals substitute for thongs in migrating from arctic to temperate to tropical climates.

The shelter differences are also due to climatic adaptions. Northern Europeans have access to forests; therefore, most construction raw materials are wood and stone. In tropical climates, the preference is for clay and bricks. Wood material is indeed undesirable in tropical climates due to termites and other insects. The roof design in the North is typically "A"-shaped to allow for snow to roll off the roof, whereas it is usually a flat roof with a gentle slope for rainwater to drain in warmer climates. The outdoors and indoors are insulated in cold climates, where one often sees the presence of a foyer as transition space. In warmer climates, indoor and outdoor boundaries are often blurred and indistinguishable. This type of housing is best typified by Spanish villas. High ceilings are most prevalent in hot and humid climates to allow air to rise. Finally, color preferences are significantly different for homes in arctic, temperate, and tropical climates.

TAKEAWAYS

- Instead of East–West differences, focus on North–South differences in consumption.

- Genes, culture, and consumption are all determined by climate zones.

- Cultural differences in punctuality, uncertainty avoidance and individualism are all reflections of climate.

REFERENCES

Diamond, Jared (1997), *Genes, Germs, and Steel*, New York: W. W. Norton.

Hall, Edward T. (1959), *The Silent Language*, New York: Doubleday.

Sheth, Jagdish N. (2017), *Genes, Climate and Consumption Culture: Connecting the Dots*, Bingley, UK: Emerald.

Sheth, Jagdish N. (2007), "Climate, Culture and Consumption: Connecting the Dots," the 12th Distinguished Faculty Lecture, February 6. Emory University.

ENTRY #54

How can you help children navigate market messages as technology progresses?

Lan Nguyen Chaplin

Associate Professor of Marketing, University of Illinois at Chicago

In 1970, the average age children started watching television was 4 years old. Jump to 2016 and the average age has gotten alarmingly younger—just 4 months old. Children's access to, and time spent using, new media is unprecedented.

Marketing messages related to critical aspects of development such as body image, gender identity, and health are disseminated across a growing number of media platforms, placing children at risk for falling prey to deceptive messages. What is concerning is that potentially misleading marketing messages are what children use to gauge self-worth, a key ingredient to their happiness and well-being.

How can we help children navigate an increasingly complex media landscape? I recommend five strategies.

1. Nurture self-esteem.
2. Foster a grateful disposition.
3. Teach prospection.
4. Encourage free play and failure.
5. Be involved and model desired behavior.

Nurture self-esteem. Self-esteem is an antecedent to materialism and risky behaviors such as sexual activity, alcohol and drug use. Why?

Regardless of income level, when children feel a void in their lives—like not fitting in or not feeling supported by parents or peers— they find ways to fill that void to boost self-worth. Material possessions are imbued with symbolic value, making them well suited for self-enhancement purposes. Engaging in risky behaviors can also be a result of an attempt to self-enhance. Therefore, it is critical that adults nurture a healthy self-esteem in children.

Foster a grateful disposition. My colleagues and I have found that encouraging adolescents to feel grateful decreases their materialistic tendencies and increases their generosity. Adults should encourage children to be grateful at an early age to buffer against overconsumption.

Teach prospection. Prospection entails acting with the future in mind, which is hard for children to do. Because marketing messages encourage immediate gratification, the ability to act with the future in mind can benefit children by aiding self-control over brand choice, risky behavior, and desires to buy. Prospection is also critical for children to be responsible social media users. Teach children to anticipate possible negative consequences of their present actions at an early age so that by the time they become frequent social media users, they will be future-minded when managing and channeling their present emotions.

Encourage free play and failure. Free play helps children develop intrinsic interests, creativity, imagination, problem solve, exert self-control, follow rules, manage emotions, and develop peer relationships, which are critical to the development of a healthy self-concept and efficacy. Allow children to play so they can experience failure, a prerequisite to learning because it motivates learners to problem-solve. The lesson children learn from playing is that you should think critically and creatively rather than assume that there is only one correct solution to a problem.

Be involved and model desired behavior. Adults should play an active role in sharing their marketplace knowledge. Adults should also remind themselves that children are watching and listening. If we want to children to exercise delay of gratification, then we should refrain from making impulse purchases.

Calls for government interventions to protect children from the daily barrage of marketing messages are valid and could potentially be helpful. However, I would argue that as caregivers and educators, we should look no further than at home and in schools to teach, inspire and empower children to be informed and responsible consumers.

TAKEAWAYS

- Look beyond the usual go-to solutions for protecting children against marketing messages such as government interventions and shielding children from media content. A healthy self-esteem, gratitude, prospection, free play, and having involved caregivers and educators will lay the foundation for children to think critically about marketing messages.

- Caregivers and educators can and should serve as primary sources of guidance for children. By being involved, sharing their marketplace knowledge and modeling desired behaviors, adults can foster social-cognitive development, empowerment and positive self-worth, which I would argue are children's best defenses against marketing messages.

REFERENCES

Chaplin, Lan Nguyen, Ronald P. Hill, and Deborah Roedder John (2014), "Poverty and Materialism: A Look at Impoverished Versus Affluent Children," *Journal of Public Policy and Marketing*, 33 (1), 78–92.

Chaplin, Lan Nguyen and Deborah Roedder John (2007), "Growing Up in a Material World: Age Differences in Materialism in Children and Adolescents," *Journal of Consumer Research*, 34 (4), 480–493.

Richins, Marsha L. and Lan Nguyen Chaplin (2015), "Material Parenting: How the Use of Goods in Parenting Fosters Materialism in the Next Generation," *Journal of Consumer Research*, 41 (6), 1333–1357.

ENTRY #55

What should students learn about marketing?

Leigh McAlister

Professor, Ed and Molly Smith Chair in Business Administration, McCombs School of Business, University of Texas at Austin

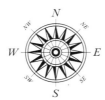

When I think of a marketing textbook, I think of a compendium of essay-like reports comprehensively covering virtually every topic ever researched by a marketing scholar. I do not recall any particular "take-away" from any of those individual essays, so, needless to say, I cannot articulate a big "take away" from the textbook as a whole, other than the fact that the textbook essays are organized into three big chunks: Situation Analysis, Strategy, 4Ps. While marketing textbooks often assert, somewhere in the text, that Strategy should reflect Situation Analysis and that 4Ps should be consistent with Strategy, the importance of those relationships is only noted in passing. In the service of comprehensive coverage, marketing textbooks flood us with detail about individual topics, but fail to give sufficient emphasis to the fact that marketing does not "work" unless the three big chunks (Situation Analysis, Strategy and 4Ps) are tightly interrelated.

The Growth Gears (Saxby and Hayes 2016; published by Advantage, Charleston, South Carolina) does the opposite. The easy to remember point of this book is that Insight (i.e., Situation Analysis), Strategy, and Execution (i.e., 4Ps) are "gears" that must be precisely aligned in order to drive growth. The authors (principals in a consulting company made up of more than 100 former CMOs from consumer, technology, B2B and service industries) target CEOs of mid-sized, operationally focused firms that want to grow. These operationally focused CEOs are constitutionally skeptical about marketing. *The Growth Gears* explains that "marketing" begins by deriving Insight (i.e., developing an understanding of customers' problems), then sets Strategy based on that insight (i.e., identifies a customer problem that the firm can solve better than competitors), and finally Executes (i.e., develops 4Ps such that every customer touchpoint reinforces the fact that the target firm solves the customer's problem better than competitors). It emphasizes that the gears must be engaged in this order. Because firms are constantly tempted to "engage gears" in a different order (i.e., to copy competitors' actions, try new media, reduce price without considering whether these interventions are consistent with Strategy), *The Growth Gears* warns against such "random acts of marketing." Such acts are likely to be inconsistent with strategy and dilutive of overall marketing impact. I fear that marketing textbooks' independent treatment of each covered topic only serves to encourage "random acts of marketing."

The Growth Gears has 224 small pages in big type; a marketing textbook, more than 700 big pages in small type. *The Growth Gears* costs less than $20; a marketing textbook, more than $200. *The Growth Gears* is a sales document—it uses marketing to sell marketing. Textbooks?

Building a course around *The Growth Gears* requires supplemental readings and cases. However, is that not also the case for building a course around a textbook? Do you find textbook coverage to be sufficient for every topic?

My students loved *The Growth Gears*. It is easy to read and persuasive. It is not only an order of magnitude cheaper than a textbook, it is an order of magnitude lighter and so less burden in their backpacks. Even more important to me, my students came away from the class (a) believing that marketing can drive growth and (b) understanding that that will only happen when the growth gears are aligned—when Strategy is built from Insight and when every marketing Execution reinforces Strategy.

TAKEAWAYS

- Read *The Growth Gears* to gain a comprehensive understanding of marketing and how it can drive growth.

REFERENCES

Saxby, A. and Hayes, P. (2016), *The Growth Gears: Using a Market-Based Framework to Drive Business Success*. Charleston, SC: Advantage.

Closing remarks

We hope you took the time to read many or most of these pearls of wisdom and agree that they have much to offer. Some may be more or less relevant depending upon your job function and knowledge base, but we believe they all have value if you dig a bit deeper, using the other materials provided by the authors.

As a quick debrief, it may be instructive to discuss the broader territories covered in the last few hundred pages. The first domain addressed *research and technology*, an area that is epitomized by change. From neuromarketing to digital marketing, we have novel ways of understanding and communicating with customers. Also, our models of the marketplace need to capture the diversity that is inherent within, and "Big Data" can help but may not currently have all the answers. Regardless, technology will continue to be integrated into marketing practice— and it will take all of our brains to understand the path ahead.

The second destination addressed *target markets and consumer behavior*. Here, we see that the ability to meaningfully know customers takes creativity and depth of thinking, as well as vigilance in avoiding the trap of assuming continuity across time or consumers. To serve our consumers, we may have to dig deep: into their underlying identities, their obligations, intuitions, relationships, and sensory experiences. We may also need to look broadly at the world in which they live, seeking to understand the dilemmas created by illiteracy and poverty.

Third is *branding*, a perennial marketing challenge. We learn here that attitudes are the centerpiece of brand identities, and that positioning strategies are impacted by people, communications, and organizational intentions that foster brand attachments. Fourth, we consider ways of *enhancing the marketplace* by dealing with perceived risk, price competition, and new product development. Further, marketers should recognize the value of partners in serving consumer needs, along with the importance of making sure customers feel welcomed and adequately served by taking a larger view of who they are and what they want.

In our fifth set of offerings, we consider *customer satisfaction*: two little words that have vast implications. These discussions run the gamut from satisficing to ultimate customer experiences, with a concentration on hearing customers' voices to determine what they really desire, in a range of areas, from price to future preferences. The sixth destination involves *consumer well-being* and focuses on subjects like food consumption, over-consumption, and health. We also learn about unintended consequences of marketing tactics and how to use marketing in the interests of the larger society.

The seventh destination is *motivating change*, considering persuasion, motivation, and association, along with physical surroundings and marketing tactics. Interestingly, these issues motivate both marketing professionals as well as consumers. The eighth and final destination is *marketing and the world at large*, which includes discussions of wisdom, collaboration, and macro-perspectives of the marketing function. Of course, it involves concerns such as sustainability, climate change, and the future of young consumers and professionals in the marketplace.

Once again, we made it under 500 words! Still, there are a few more global takeaways to consider:

- Marketing professionals must be ready for change. For example, media vehicles that exist today may not be here tomorrow since each new generation redefines what it means to be "connected." The media consumers "watch" or attend to is rapidly redefining what successful marketing communications are.
- Consumers are complex in their backgrounds and preferences. They are becoming increasingly diverse and understanding who they are and what they want cannot be taken for granted. For instance, they value branded items, but what makes for successful brand identities requires considerable research and deliberation.
- Marketing is about relationship-building through satisfying experiences. Marketers need to develop long-lasting associations with consumers and a variety of internal and external partners that must come together for product delivery. What they want may or may not be obvious or easily provided. Conflict can result, but its resolution is one road to success.
- Marketing can make the world a better place. From meeting essential needs in the marketplace to helping solve large societal problems, marketers have the capability to understand and develop goods and services that meet most desires. Finding ways of delivering them to the right people at the right time and at the right price is what we do.

With all we know about good marketing practice, we will never know enough. Even if marketers could create near-certainty about what to do and when to do it, the "unknown unknowns" and unintended consequences will still catch us by surprise. The final lesson is to plan as best you can to take advantage of opportunities in the future, but keep your eyes wide open for the unexpected that may require a change of direction.

And as you go, share with others. The lessons you learn—inside or outside your own trenches—can help others navigate a changing world, both in the domain of marketing and beyond.

Index

access to markets 47
Activity Data 19
additive error component 12, 13
adult self-control 7
advertising concept 52
advertising effects 63–64
Ajzen, Icek 51
Amazon's Dash Replenishment service 22
antismoking and anti-marijuana ads 122
Argo, Jennifer J. 151
asymmetric attraction effects 74
asymmetric line-extension effects 74
asymmetric price competition 73–74
attitude: definition 51; influential theory 51; "rub off" advertisement 51–52; structural equation analysis 52
attraction effects 73–74
attractive models 121
attribution models 113
"authenticity" 28
autonomy-threatening rules 7

Bart, Yakov 4
behavioral change 29, 151
behavioral modifications 144
Berry, Len 115
big data 15–16: applications 100; business processes and customer connections 100; cognitive and emotional mechanisms 102; data privacy and personal information security 100–101; marketing research techniques 101; transparency and control 101

bioscience: autonomy-threatening rules 7; consumer-policy perspective 7; human traits and behavior, causal models 6; libertarian paternalism 7; self-control 6–7; social policy 6
black community 9
body-esteem threats 131
"Borrowed interest" 54
bottom-up approach 47
brand-owned type 113
brand-related decisions 54–55
brands: attitude 51–52; communication effects 54–55; exercise routine 66; Gatorade sticker 66; multi-attribute model (MAM) 51; self-efficacy 67
business collaboration 168–169
business macromarketing 171–173
business relationships: bad history 83; customization 83; grand gestures 82–83; mutual customers and stakeholders 83; pie-expansion work 83; trust 82

Cameron, Douglas 32
career motivation 159–160
Chae, Inyoung 4
children's access, market messages 180–181: desired behavior 181; free play and failure 181; grateful disposition 181; prospection 181
children's self-control 7
Chitturi, Ravi 38
cigarette ads 121
climate 177–178
clothing 131–132
Cohen, Ben 174

Coleman, Nicole Verrochi 86
communal self-expansion experiences 21
communication effects 54–55
competing ads category 54
competitive market 13
compliance barriers 147
confidence intervals 12
conjunctive model 103
constraining experiences 21
Consumer Culture Theory (CCT) 32
consumer-device assemblage 22
consumer-policy perspective 7
consumers: advertising effects 63–64; antismoking and anti-marijuana ads 122; attractive models 121; "authenticity" 28; behavioral change 29; behavior-change strategy 151; brands see brands;.cigarette ads 121; compliance barriers 147; consumption contexts 37; culture theory 63; decisions making 34–35; "dissociative" reference groups 150, 151; economists 104; elements 27; environmental factors 154–155; experience and response 40–41; features 38, 39; female mannequins 133–134; fixed discount rate 144; future preferences 106–107; goals 153; identity loyalty 28–29; individual identity 28; innovative technology 142; intra-identity conflict 28; low-literate and low-income 46–47; M-A-P segmentation approach 148; "more fun = less functional" intuition 38; motivation 141–142; multiple target markets 27; National Association of Retired Plan Participants (NARPP) 148; neutral association 151; "personality"/"psychographics" 28; persuasion enhancement 147; photo-taking effect 156–157; Population Services International (PSI) 147; pricing 109–111; product quality 16, 38; public policy advocates 28; resources scarcity 153; scent effect 43–44; self-esteem 28; sports utility vehicle (SUV) 28; stereotypes 68–70; voluntary medical male circumcision

(VMMC) 147–148; welfare 79; "work-related"/"functional" products 37
consumption contexts 37, 178
coordinated media 55
Coskuner-Balli, Gokcen 32
cost reduction 58
cultivation theory 64
Cultural Deviant Model 10
culture-consistent consumption behaviors 90
culture theory 63, 178
customer-owned type 113
customer satisfaction 16, 97
customer service: "emotional spillover" 92; firm controls 91; frontline employees (FLEs) 91; Organizational Frontlines Research (OFR) group 92
customers ultimate experience 112–113
cutting-edge digital marketing phenomena 4

Dahl, Darren W. 151
data capturing, life decisions 18–19
decision comfort approach 104
decision making 34–35, 146: ethical decision making 86; immediate feelings 145; individual choice 85; psychological health 85. see also consumers; food decision making
digital marketing: cutting-edge digital marketing phenomena 4;mobile advertising field experiment data 4; mobile devices and social media 3;purchase decision process 4; seeded marketing campaigns 4; word-of-mouth (WOM) marketing 4
DINESERVE 116
discount retailers 15
"dissociative" reference groups 150, 151
diversity: black community 9; Cultural Deviant Model 10; heterogeneity identification 11; homogeneity 9; monolithic segments 10; multicultural consumers 9, 10; primary marketing journals 9; racial/ethnic minority segments 9

diversity-related behaviors 89
diversity seeking scale 88–90

economic agents 31
economists 104
education/financial resources 46
entrepreneurs, elements 47
environmental sustainability 61
equity-building benefits 57–58
ethical decision making 86
ethnic-oriented products 88
executional variables, advertising effects 63
expectancy theory 64
exposure time, brand 54

fashion retailers 133
"faux-diversity" 89
female mannequins 133–134
financial resources 47
financial services 68
Fishbein, Martin 51
fixed discount rate 144
food decision making: complexities of 129; environments 128; portion sizes 128; pricing 127–128; taste and health factors 127
food packaging 125: designs 130–131
food portion sizes 124
Fournier, Susan 32
Franklin, Ben 135
frontline employees (FLEs) 91
frontline service see customer service
functional (problem-solving) solutions 58

gentrification 89
Gentry, James W. 104
Gilovich, Tom 98
global-marketing-commons 172
graphic health warnings (GHWs) 135–136
Growth Gears, The 183–184

Hawes, Kelly L. 104
Hayes, Pete 183
healthy food marketing: lose–lose scenario 124; packaging 125; pleasure 125; portion sizes 124

heterogeneity identification 11
higher-quality (HQ) brands' price 73–74
higher-quality line extension (HQE) 74
Holt, Douglas 32
homogeneity identification 9
human behavior see bioscience

immediate feelings 145
individual identity 28
influencer marketing 4
informational interventions 80
innovation process 60
innovative technology 142
Internet of Things (IoT) 21–22
intra-identity conflict 28

Keinan, Anat 98
Korschun, Daniel 175
Krishna, Aradhna 43

large-scale correlation analysis 177
lay theories 34
Lehmann, Donald 104
LibQUAL 116
life satisfaction 98
line-extension effects 73–74
literacy 131
LODGSERV 116
Loewenstein, George 103
long-term memory banks 44
lower equity brands 60–61
lower-quality (LQ) brands' price 73–74
lower-quality line extension (LQE) 74
low-income consumer 46–47
low-literate consumer 46–47
loyalty and brand advocacy behaviors 58

machine learning 18
macromarketing 171–173
M-A-P segmentation approach 148
marketing messages 180
marketing research techniques 101
marketplace literacy program 47
Marketsphere Earth 171
mobile advertising field experiment data 4

"model minority" stereotype 64
motivation 141–142
multi-attribute model (MAM) 51
multicultural consumers 9, 10
multiple target markets 27

National Association of Retired Plan
    Participants (NARPP) 148
need-for-touch (NFT) 40
neutral association 151
Nikolova, Hristina 85, 86
non-compensatory behavior models 13
normative decision theory 103, 104

online shopping 41
Organizational Frontlines Research
    (OFR) group 92
over-consumption 130

Parasuraman, Parsu 115
Parker, Jeffrey 104
partner-owned type 113
"personality"/"psychographics" 28
persuasion enhancement 147
photo-taking effect 156–157
policy debates 64
Population Services International (PSI)
    147
post-purchase 112
Poynor, Cait 104
pre-purchase 112
preventive education 135–137
price 109–111: competition 73–74;
    elasticity 13; food decision making
    127–128
product/service category 54
product-specific lay theories 34, 35
product's strength guarantee 36
psychological ownership 41
psychological relationship-based factors
    58
public policy advocates 28
purchase 112

quality 16, 38

regression models 12
resource-constrained environments 47
resources scarcity 153

retrieval cues advertisement 55
risk 79–80
"rub off" advertisement 51–52

Sarvary, Miklos 4
Sawyer, Tom 37
Saxby, Art 183
scented products 43–44
scent effect 43–44
scent, memory aid 43–44
seeded marketing campaigns 4
self-control 6–7
self-defeating consumption 6–7
self-efficacy 136
self-esteem 28, 180–181
self-evident remedies 79
self-extension experiences 21
Sen, Sankar 175
sense-of-community 89
service quality 115–116
SERVQUAL 115–116
signatures, brand 55
Simon, Herb 103
Simpson, Bonnie 151
Situation Analysis, Strategy, 4Ps 183
smart devices interactions 21: decision
    making 22
social bonds 31
social and consumption dynamics 89
social/independent/external type 113
social-policy perspective 6, 7
sports utility vehicle (SUV) 28
stereotypes 68–70
structural behavior models 13
structural equation analysis 52
subsistence marketplaces 46–47
success: breathing space 77; catchiness
    77; challenges 60–61; idea 76;
    innovator offers 76; "permission,"
    new products 77; stickiness 77;
    support 77
"sufferfests" success 97
sustainability initiatives 174–176
sustainable products 35, 47
systemic marketing exchange 171

target market, identification: Consumer
    Culture Theory (CCT) 32; economic
    agents 31; informed consumer 31;

social bonds 31; transformative process 32
Thompson, Craig J. 31, 32
Transformative Consumer Research 130
transformative process 32
Tweet2Quit 122
two-stage model 12, 13

unplanned/impulse purchase 41
unscented products 43–44
Üstüner, Tuba 31

voluntary medical male circumcision (VMMC) 147–148

welfare 79
White, Katherine 151
wisdom 165–166
word-of-mouth (WOM) marketing 4
"work-related" / "functional" products 37

Xie, Yi 104

Yao, Dai 4

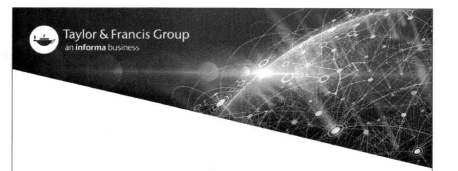

Taylor & Francis eBooks

www.taylorfrancis.com

A single destination for eBooks from Taylor & Francis with increased functionality and an improved user experience to meet the needs of our customers.

90,000+ eBooks of award-winning academic content in Humanities, Social Science, Science, Technology, Engineering, and Medical written by a global network of editors and authors.

TAYLOR & FRANCIS EBOOKS OFFERS:

- A streamlined experience for our library customers
- A single point of discovery for all of our eBook content
- Improved search and discovery of content at both book and chapter level

REQUEST A FREE TRIAL
support@taylorfrancis.com